The Boundaries Bible - The Antidote to Burnout

Jonathan Riley

Published by Jonathan Riley, 2024.

While every precaution has been taken in the preparation of this book, the publisher assumes no responsibility for errors or omissions, or for damages resulting from the use of the information contained herein.

THE BOUNDARIES BIBLE - THE ANTIDOTE TO BURNOUT

First edition. February 18, 2024.

Copyright © 2024 Jonathan Riley.

ISBN: 979-8224852468

Written by Jonathan Riley.

Table of Contents

"Beyond Burnout: A Guide to Setting Healthy Boundaries with Work"

Table of Contents

Chapter 1: Understanding Boundaries in the Workplace

Chapter 2: Exploring the Impact of Boundaries and Burnout

Chapter 3: Identifying Your Boundaries

Chapter 4: Assessing Your Current Work-Life Balance

Chapter 5: Thriving in the Digital Age

Chapter 6: Communicating Your Boundaries

Chapter 7: Communicating Your Boundaries with Others

Chapter 8: Setting Boundaries with Remote Work

Chapter 9: Managing Boundary Violations

Chapter 10: Boundary Setting and Self-Awareness

How To Use This Workbook

Welcome to the "Setting Healthy Boundaries with Work Workbook." This workbook is intended to serve as a practical guide to help you establish and maintain healthy boundaries in your professional life. This book provides easy-to-understand information and practical examples to help you set and maintain healthy boundaries in your personal and professional relationships.

This workbook is written in a topical form to provide a step-by-step approach to understanding and implementing healthy boundaries with work. Each chapter focuses on a specific aspect of boundaries, including identifying boundaries, setting boundaries, communicating boundaries, and enforcing boundaries. Additionally, each chapter is followed by a set of questions to help you reflect on what you have learned and apply it to your life.

For those who have no boundaries or struggle with setting and maintaining them, this book is an excellent resource. It is written in a concise and easy-to-read format, making it a great option for those who may not have much time to read. The practical examples and questions after each chapter will help you apply what you learn to your own life.

To get the most out of this book, it is recommend that you read each chapter thoroughly and take the time to answer the questions provided. Reflect on how you can apply what you have learned to your life, and be honest with yourself about any challenges or obstacles you may face along the way.

Remember that establishing healthy boundaries is a process, and it may take time to get it right. Be patient with yourself and don't be afraid to ask for help or support when needed. With practice and perseverance, you can successfully set and maintain healthy boundaries in your life and improve your overall well-being.

Introduction

In today's fast-paced world, technology has made it easier for us to stay connected and work round the clock, leading to an increasing challenge in finding a work-life balance. This issue is further compounded as more and more employees work remotely, emphasizing the importance of establishing clear boundaries between work and personal life.

The importance of setting healthy boundaries cannot be overstated. Research has shown that setting boundaries allows you to maintain a work-life balance, avoid burnout, and improve your overall well-being (Greenhaus & Beutell, 1985). By setting boundaries, you give yourself the space to focus on personal priorities, reduce stress, and enhance your relationships with colleagues, friends, and family. Moreover, setting healthy boundaries promotes productivity and fosters a sense of control and self-worth, which can ultimately contribute to a happier and more fulfilling life (Kossek & Lautsch, 2018).

Setting healthy boundaries is essential for maintaining a work-life balance and avoiding burnout. Burnout, a state of emotional, physical, and mental exhaustion resulting from prolonged and excessive stress, can have significant consequences such as reduced productivity, decreased job satisfaction, and health problems. Research indicates that burnout rates have been on the rise, with a 2020 study showing that 76% of US employees experienced burnout at least sometimes, and 28% reported feeling burned out "very often" or "always" (Gallop, 2020).

In the competitive job market we face today, employers are constantly seeking ways to cut costs and boost productivity. Consequently, we often find ourselves taking on extra tasks and responsibilities without the necessary support or resources. This can create overwhelming feelings and a sense of being perpetually on the verge of burnout. The relentless pressure to meet deadlines, achieve targets, and perform at a high level can lead to burnout as we struggle to keep up with the demands of our jobs.

The drive to achieve and excel is a major contributor to burnout, with many people feeling they must consistently outperform their peers to succeed. This constant need to prove oneself can strain our mental and physical well-being. Failure to establish a healthy work-life balance can exacerbate burnout. Many find ourselves working long hours, responding to emails and messages outside of work, and incessantly checking in with our managers and colleagues. This unrelenting pressure to be available can cause exhaustion and burnout. The expectation for employees to be available 24/7 only makes it more difficult to disconnect from work and find balance.

Fortunately, setting boundaries can help prevent burnout and enhance your overall well-being. By defining your limits and communicating them clearly, you can foster a healthier work environment and reduce stress.

In this workbook, we will guide you through the process of setting healthy boundaries with work. We will discuss the benefits of boundaries, common boundary violations, and strategies for setting and communicating your boundaries effectively. You will learn how to identify your values and priorities, create a boundary plan, and communicate your boundaries to your colleagues and managers.

We hope that this workbook will empower you to establish healthy boundaries with work and achieve a more balanced and fulfilling life. Our goal is to provide practical tools and strategies that you can use to improve your well-being and thrive in your career.

So let's get started!

Chapter 1: Understanding Boundaries in the Workplace

"Boundaries protect the inner core of your identity and your integrity. Without them, you are at the mercy of the world." - Dr. John Lee

What Are Boundaries?

Boundaries are the invisible yet essential barriers that delineate and safeguard our personal space, encompassing both physical and emotional realms. They are foundational to forging and maintaining healthy relationships, as well as fostering a strong sense of self. Boundaries enable us to articulate our needs, preferences, and limits effectively, ensuring we receive the respect and consideration we deserve. They can be applied across various contexts, including friendships, romantic relationships, family dynamics, and workplace interactions.

At their essence, boundaries function as a protective mechanism for self-preservation and self-respect for all of us. They equip us with the power to shield our emotional and physical well-being by delineating the acceptable and unacceptable behaviors, actions, and situations we may encounter. Establishing clear boundaries is a vital life skill, as it empowers us to maintain autonomy, control, and self-worth. By setting personal boundaries, we can avert manipulation, mistreatment, or becoming overwhelmed by the demands and expectations of others.

Boundaries are not one-size-fits-all constructs; they are highly individualized and dynamic. They can differ significantly among people and may be influenced by factors such as cultural background, social norms, personal values, and past experiences. Boundaries can also evolve and change over time, as our personal circumstances, relationships, and priorities shift. This adaptability enables us to establish boundaries that best serve our needs and well-being at any given moment.

Communication is central to the successful establishment and maintenance of boundaries for all of us. Effectively conveying our needs, preferences, and limits requires clarity, assertiveness, and respect. It is crucial to recognize our personal values, needs, and limits and express them transparently and respectfully to others. This process may involve negotiation and compromise to arrive at mutually agreeable boundaries.

It is essential to remember that establishing boundaries does not equate to being rigid, inflexible, or selfish. On the contrary, setting healthy boundaries demonstrates a commitment to self-care and self-respect, which in turn, allows for more balanced and fulfilling relationships. Respecting and honoring the boundaries of others is equally important, as it fosters an environment of mutual understanding, empathy, and respect.

Furthermore, self-awareness plays a significant role in setting effective boundaries for all of us. Being mindful of our emotional state, personal values, and past experiences can help us identify areas where we may need to establish or adjust our boundaries. Reflecting on personal experiences and learning from past boundary-related challenges can inform future boundary-setting decisions, ultimately contributing to personal growth and well-being.

Boundaries are the cornerstone of cultivating healthy relationships and safeguarding our emotional, physical, and intellectual well-being. By setting and maintaining clear boundaries, we can create a robust sense of self, forge respectful and balanced relationships, and achieve a harmonious work-life balance. Continuously honing boundary-setting skills is a lifelong journey that enriches personal growth, self-respect, and overall well-being for all of us.

The Role of Values in Setting Boundaries

Boundaries are essential in maintaining a healthy work-life balance, and our values play a critical role in the process of setting and maintaining these boundaries. Our values represent what we hold most important in life, and they act as a guiding compass when it comes to making decisions and setting priorities. By understanding and identifying our core values, we can set boundaries that are in alignment with our beliefs, ensuring that we protect our well-being and live a more fulfilling life.

Core values are the fundamental beliefs and principles that guide our actions, decisions, and behaviors. They are deeply ingrained within us and are shaped by various factors, such as upbringing, culture, personal experiences, and relationships. To set effective boundaries, it is vital to first identify our core values, as they provide the foundation for boundary-setting. Some examples of core values include honesty, respect, family, integrity, and autonomy.

Taking some time to reflect on what truly matters to you is an essential step in identifying your core values. Consider what principles or beliefs are most important to you, and think about when you feel most fulfilled and satisfied with your life. Additionally, it's helpful to recognize the values you admire in others and understand why they resonate with you. Reflecting on your experiences and pondering these questions can help you develop a clearer understanding of your core values and the role they play in your life.

Once you have identified your core values, it is essential to align your boundaries with these values. Aligning your values and boundaries helps ensure that you are living in accordance with your beliefs and priorities, which contributes to a greater sense of well-being and satisfaction. For example, if one of your core values is family, you might set boundaries around work hours and technology use to ensure that you have quality time with your loved ones. If you value self-care, you might establish a boundary that reserves a specific amount of time each day or week for activities that nourish your body, mind, and spirit.

Reviewing your core values and determining how they relate to different aspects of your life, such as work, relationships, and self-care, is an important step in aligning your values with your boundaries. Identify specific boundaries that support your values and priorities, ensuring that they are clear, realistic, and achievable. Develop a plan to implement these boundaries, taking into account potential challenges and obstacles, as well as strategies for overcoming them.

Our values have a significant impact on the boundaries we set and how effectively we maintain them. When our boundaries are rooted in our values, we are more likely to feel motivated and committed to upholding them, even in the face of external pressures or challenges. Values-based boundaries promote a greater sense of authenticity, as they reflect who we truly are and what we believe in. When our boundaries align with our values, we are better able to navigate difficult situations, make decisions that serve our best interests, and cultivate a more balanced and fulfilling life.

Our core values play a crucial role in setting and maintaining healthy boundaries. By identifying and aligning our values with our boundaries, we can create a life that is congruent with our beliefs and priorities, fostering a greater sense of well-being, satisfaction, and personal fulfillment.

Why Should I Set Boundaries with Work?

Creating boundaries in the workplace is an essential exercise that safeguards us from the risks of burnout by facilitating a sense of control over our time and energy. These boundaries enable us to prioritize our responsibilities and direct our focus towards the most crucial tasks, ultimately preventing us from overextending ourselves.

In the context of our interactions with clients, colleagues, and superiors, setting boundaries plays a pivotal role in fostering a professional and harmonious work atmosphere. Clear demarcation of roles and responsibilities eliminates confusion and miscommunication, promoting mutual understanding of expectations. Such clarity enhances the efficiency of our work, minimizes potential disputes, and fosters an environment of mutual respect, thereby strengthening professional relationships and facilitating effective collaboration.

Recent studies highlight the critical role of boundary-setting in preventing occupational burnout. For instance, a research published in the Journal of Occupational Health Psychology illustrates that employees who create a clear distinction between work and personal life experience less fatigue and more work-family enrichment compared to those who do not (Shockley et al., 2017). Moreover, setting boundaries contributes to maintaining a healthy work-life balance, which is paramount for our physical and mental health. This fact is evidenced by an American Psychological Association survey, indicating that over a third of American workers experience chronic work stress, potentially leading to adverse health effects (American Psychological Association, 2017). Thus, by creating and adhering to these boundaries, we can better care for ourselves and mitigate the harmful impacts of chronic stress.

Consider the case of Jessica, a diligent marketing manager at a bustling startup. Passionate about her job and the company's mission, Jessica frequently found herself working long hours, constantly replying to work emails throughout the day and night. This perpetual connection to her work began to adversely affect her mental and physical well-being. Realizing the need for change, Jessica decided to establish boundaries around her work schedule and communication. She negotiated with her manager to stop checking her work emails after 5pm and dedicated specific time slots for self-care activities such as exercise and meditation. By treating these self-care appointments with the same importance as her work meetings, Jessica began to experience increased energy and focus during her work hours, ultimately improving her productivity. Her stress and anxiety levels decreased, and she felt more at ease, knowing that she had designated times to disconnect from work and concentrate on other aspects of her life. Over time, her colleagues started respecting her boundaries, easing the pressure of constant availability. By setting and upholding these boundaries, Jessica successfully maintained a healthy work-life balance and improved her overall well-being.

The establishment of work boundaries not only enhances our work life but also significantly impacts our overall health and well-being. Creating a distinct separation between our professional and personal lives minimizes the risk of chronic stress, which can lead to various physical and mental health issues. Furthermore, setting boundaries ensures that we have the necessary time and space to engage in self-care activities vital for our physical and mental health, thereby increasing our overall happiness, resilience, and well-being.

Achieving a work-life balance is crucial for our overall well-being, and setting boundaries is key to this endeavor. By delineating clear lines between our professional and personal lives, we can effectively allocate our time and energy. This balance allows us to feel more fulfilled in our careers while also nurturing our personal lives and relationships outside of work. Moreover, a healthy work-life balance can positively impact our job satisfaction and performance, leading us to approach our work with positivity and heightened motivation, which in turn can lead to greater success and satisfaction in our professional endeavors.

The significance of setting work boundaries cannot be overstated. By doing so, we promote a healthy work-life balance, enhance our mental and physical health, and boost our productivity levels. By setting these clear boundaries with clients, colleagues, and managers, we cultivate a respectful and efficient work atmosphere, positively influencing both our personal and professional lives. Jessica's experience serves as a prime example of how setting and maintaining boundaries can stave off burnout, improve overall well-being, and elevate the quality of life.

Establishing work boundaries is an essential strategy for achieving a healthy work-life balance and avoiding burnout. By effectively communicating our limitations, we can manage our time and energy more efficiently, thereby improving our overall well-being and productivity. More than just a strategy, setting boundaries paves the way for a sustainable work environment, offering positive ramifications for both our personal and professional lives.

The Consequences of Not Setting Boundaries

Boundaries are an essential aspect of any healthy relationship, including the one we have with our work. They define what we are willing to accept and what we are not willing to tolerate. Without boundaries, we are more likely to experience burnout, decreased productivity, negative impacts on relationships, and negative impacts on our health.

When we don't set boundaries, we open ourselves up to burnout. People who experience burnout often feel like they have nothing left to give and are unable to meet the demands of their work. Not setting boundaries in the workplace can contribute to burnout by allowing stress to build up over time. When we don't set boundaries, we are more likely to take on more work than we can handle and become overwhelmed.

Not setting boundaries can also lead to a lack of focus and motivation. When we don't set boundaries, we are more likely to be pulled in multiple directions at once. We may find ourselves constantly switching between tasks and not completing any of them. This can lead to a decrease in productivity and a sense of dissatisfaction with our work. Furthermore, not setting boundaries can lead to being taken advantage of by our co-workers. We may find ourselves being asked to do more than our fair share of work or being expected to be available at all times. This can lead to resentment and can damage our relationships with our co-workers. Not setting boundaries can also have a negative impact on our relationships outside of work. We may find ourselves neglecting our friends and family in favour of work.

When we do not set boundaries, we are more likely to experience stress and anxiety, which can be detrimental to our health. Stress can lead to a variety of physical and mental health problems, such as high blood pressure, heart disease, and depression. Lack of boundaries can also lead to poor sleeping habits, which can have a negative impact on our physical and mental health. Burnout, decreased productivity, negative impacts on relationships, and negative impacts on health are all consequences of not setting boundaries.

It is important to set boundaries to maintain a healthy work-life balance. While setting boundaries may be difficult, it is necessary for our well-being. Taking the time to identify our personal and professional boundaries and communicating them effectively is essential. Prioritizing self-care can help us set healthy boundaries and maintain a good work-life balance by ensuring that we are in good physical and mental health.

The Power of Setting Boundaries

Setting boundaries is an essential part of achieving a healthy and productive work-life balance. By understanding the benefits of setting boundaries and learning how to set and maintain them, we can create a more positive and satisfying work environment. Discover the benefits of boundary-setting and how it can positively impact your work and personal life.

1. Improved work-life balance: Setting boundaries allows you to separate work from other aspects of your life, such as your family and personal time. By making a conscious effort to disconnect from work during non-work hours, you can enjoy a more balanced life and reduce stress.

2. Reduced stress and burnout: When we don't set boundaries, we can become overwhelmed by the demands of our job. This can lead to feelings of burnout, which can negatively impact our mental and physical health. By setting boundaries, we can better manage our workload and reduce stress.

3. Increased productivity and focus: When we set boundaries, we create a more structured environment that allows us to focus on the task at hand. This can result in increased productivity and better quality work.

4. Better time management: Setting boundaries allows us to prioritize our tasks and manage our time more effectively. By focusing on the most important tasks first, we can use our time more efficiently and achieve our goals more quickly.

5. Improved relationships with co-workers: Setting boundaries can improve communication and understanding between colleagues and managers. When we assert ourselves and communicate our needs clearly, we can create a more positive and productive work environment.

6. Greater ability to prioritize and achieve goals: Setting boundaries allows us to focus on what is most important, both at work and in our personal lives. This can help us achieve our goals more effectively and lead to greater success.

7. Increased job satisfaction and well-being: When we set boundaries, we take control of our work environment and make it more manageable. This can lead to increased job satisfaction and overall well-being.

8. More time for self-care and personal development: Setting boundaries allows us to make time for self-care and personal development, which can help us maintain good mental and physical health.

9. Better communication and assertiveness skills: Setting boundaries requires us to communicate our needs clearly and assertively. This can improve our communication and assertiveness skills and make us more effective in all aspects of our lives.

10. Greater respect and understanding from others: When we set boundaries, we communicate that we value ourselves and our time. This can result in greater respect and understanding from others, both at work and in our personal lives.

Remember to be clear about your boundaries, communicate them effectively, and stand by them. With practice, setting boundaries will become second nature and will greatly benefit your overall well-being.

Boundaries Assessment

This assessment is designed to help you gain insight into how your work is impacting your overall well-being. By taking this assessment, you'll be able to gain insight into how your work is impacting your overall well-being and take control of your work-life balance.

Please answer the following questions using the scale provided below:

1 - Strongly Disagree 2 - Disagree 3 - Neutral 4 - Agree 5 - Strongly Agree

1. I often feel emotionally exhausted at work.
2. My free time is difficult to enjoy due to work-related stress.
3. My work seems pointless or unimportant to me.
4. Work-related stress makes it hard for me to enjoy my family life.
5. I experience a sense of cynicism or negativity towards my job.
6. My social life suffers due to work-related stress and exhaustion.
7. Coping with the demands of my job is challenging for me.
8. Separating work from my personal life is difficult.
9. I feel that I am not respected in my work environment.

10. I lack support from my colleagues or supervisors at work.
11. Work often forces me to sacrifice personal or leisure time.
12. Self-care activities like exercise, healthy eating, and relaxation are difficult to prioritize.
13. My sleep or rest is negatively impacted by work.
14. Expressing my needs and concerns to others at work is challenging.
15. Effectively managing my workload is something I struggle with.
16. Asking for help at work is something I'm uncomfortable with.
17. I no longer enjoy activities or hobbies I used to love due to work.
18. Work causes me to feel irritable, impatient, or easily frustrated.
19. My job contributes to feelings of depression, anxiety, or stress.
20. My job doesn't align with my values or goals.

Interpretation

Add up your total score and refer to the following scale:

20-40: Healthy Boundaries - This range suggests that you have healthy work-life boundaries. You are generally able to separate work from your personal life, and work-related stress doesn't significantly impact your emotional wellbeing or enjoyment of life. Keep maintaining these boundaries, and be mindful of any changes.

41-60: Mild Boundary Issues - This range indicates that you may have some issues with work-life balance. While you generally have good boundaries, there might be times when work stress affects your personal life. Consider seeking strategies to further improve your boundaries and stress management.

61-80: Moderate Boundary Issues - This score suggests that you're experiencing moderate boundary issues. Work stress may be regularly seeping into your personal life, and possibly affecting your mood and overall wellbeing. It's important to take steps to address these issues, which might include discussing your workload with a supervisor or seeking support from a mental health professional.

81-100: Significant Boundary Issues - This score suggests significant issues with work-life balance. You may frequently feel stressed or overwhelmed by work, and it seems to significantly impact your personal life and emotional health. It's crucial to seek help, such as speaking to a supervisor about your workload or seeking support from a mental health professional.

Above 100: Severe Boundary Issues - This range suggests that your work is severely affecting your personal life and wellbeing. You might often feel stressed, exhausted, and negative towards your job. You might also struggle to enjoy your free time due to work-related stress. It's crucial to seek immediate help, either by discussing these issues with a supervisor or seeking support from a mental health professional.

After completing this assessment, you will have a better understanding of how your work is impacting your overall well-being. The results will provide you with an indication of the level of burnout you may be experiencing and offer guidance on how to address it. This will empower you to take control of your work-life balance and maintain your mental and physical well-being.

Self-Assessment: Understanding Boundaries in the Workplace

The purpose of this self-assessment is to help you reflect on your current understanding, practice, and effectiveness of setting and maintaining boundaries. By answering the following questions, you will be able to gauge your current standing and identify areas for potential improvement. Remember, this is a tool for self-improvement and learning; there are no 'right' or 'wrong' answers.

Please answer the following questions using the scale provided below:

1 - Strongly Disagree 2 - Disagree 3 - Neutral 4 - Agree 5 - Strongly Agree

1. I have a clear understanding of the different types of boundaries.
2. My personal values play an important role in shaping my work boundaries.
3. I recognize the importance of setting boundaries in a professional environment.

4. I am aware of the potential negative consequences of not setting boundaries.
5. I believe that setting boundaries can improve my relationships with colleagues and supervisors.
6. I feel comfortable setting boundaries to protect my well-being.
7. I often consider how my personal values align with my workplace boundaries.
8. I have experienced positive outcomes as a result of setting boundaries.
9. I understand that not setting boundaries can lead to increased stress and burnout.
10. I am confident in my ability to set and maintain boundaries.
11. I can identify situations where setting boundaries has helped me manage my workload more effectively.
12. I actively work on setting boundaries to prevent being overwhelmed by work demands.
13. I feel that my current work boundaries are appropriate and effective.
14. I am open to adjusting my boundaries based on changes in my work environment or personal life.
15. I communicate my boundaries clearly to my co-workers and supervisors.
16. I can effectively enforce my boundaries when necessary.
17. I am willing to seek help or guidance when facing challenges related to setting boundaries at work.
18. I recognize the power of setting boundaries in promoting a healthier and more productive work environment.
19. I am committed to continuous improvement and growth in my boundary-setting skills.
20. I understand the role of boundaries in contributing to my overall well-being and job satisfaction.

Interpretation

Add up your total score and refer to the following scale:

20-40: You may need to work on understanding and setting boundaries in the workplace. Consider seeking guidance or resources to improve your boundary-setting skills.

41-60: You have some understanding of workplace boundaries but could benefit from further exploration and development of your boundary-setting skills.

61-80: You have a good understanding of boundaries in the workplace and are actively working on setting and maintaining them. Continue refining your skills and adapting to changes in your work environment.

81-100: You demonstrate a strong understanding of workplace boundaries and are effective in setting and maintaining them. Keep up the good work and continue to prioritize your well-being in the workplace.

Use your score as a guide to areas requiring attention or further development. Regardless of your score, remember that setting healthy boundaries is an ongoing process. Let this assessment guide you towards a balanced professional life.

Exercise: Understanding Boundaries in the Workplace

1. Can you identify a situation where not setting boundaries led to negative consequences for you?
2. How does setting boundaries contribute to a healthier and more productive work environment?
3. Can you recall a time when setting a boundary helped you manage your workload better?
4. How do boundaries protect your well-being in the workplace?
5. In what ways can I better distinguish between work time and personal time?
6. What are some of the potential negative consequences if I don't enforce my boundaries at work?
7. How can I align my personal values with my work boundaries more effectively?
8. Are there any specific work tasks that consistently infringe upon

my personal time? How can I address these?

9. What strategies can I use to manage my workload more effectively, in accordance with my boundaries?

10. In what ways can setting boundaries improve my relationships with others?

11. Are there any changes in my work environment or personal life that require me to adjust my boundaries

12. Are there any situations where I feel uncomfortable or stressed due to a lack of boundaries? How can I address these?

Chapter 2: Exploring the Impact of Boundaries and Burnout

"Boundaries are the armor that protect us from the flames of burnout."

– Jonathan Riley

An Overview of Burnout

Exploring the realm of our lives, we often encounter a blurred line between our professional and personal worlds. This blurred line, which is frequently made unclear by connectivity's constant buzz and expectations to always be "on," plants a pervasive sense of imbalance and a distressing lack of control in our lives. This unending cycle, if left unchecked, can result in the state of total exhaustion known as burnout.

Burnout, a term that has gained substantial recognition in recent years, is not simply about feeling overworked or stressed. Rather, it is a complex, multifaceted state of physical, emotional, and mental exhaustion, triggered by prolonged stress and unmet expectations. It is a state that creeps in slowly, not always discernible in its early stages, but whose impact is profound, affecting our health, relationships, productivity, and overall quality of life.

Understanding burnout involves recognizing its varied types and stages. Emotional burnout, for instance, is characterized by feelings of emotional depletion, detachment, and a reduced sense of accomplishment. Physical burnout, on the other hand, is marked by chronic fatigue, sleep disturbances, and other physical symptoms. There is also cognitive burnout, reflected in impaired concentration, forgetfulness, and diminished creativity.

Stages of burnout progress over time, often starting subtly with feelings of tension and strain, before escalating to chronic exhaustion, cynicism, and feelings of inefficacy. The early warning signs might be as subtle as persistent fatigue, irritability, or a sense of being overwhelmed. If recognized early, addressing the root causes of these symptoms can help prevent the progression to full-blown burnout.

One of the primary contributors to burnout is a lack of boundaries. In our always-connected world, we often find ourselves overcommitted, constantly under pressure, and grappling with unrealistic expectations. The boundaries between work and personal life blur, creating a feeling of being always "on". This not only depletes our energy reserves but also robs us of the much-needed personal time to recharge and rejuvenate.

This lack of boundaries can be further exacerbated by the expectations we set for ourselves, and those set by others. When we fail to delineate our limits, we risk overextending ourselves to meet demands that are not only unsustainable but also harmful to our well-being.

How, then, can we counteract this boundary-less existence and potential burnout? The answer lies in cultivating a healthier, more sustainable lifestyle. This involves setting clear, firm boundaries between work and personal life, and being assertive in maintaining these boundaries. It requires us to prioritize our well-being, engage in self-care practices, and nurture our physical, emotional, and mental health.

The exploration of the impact of boundaries and burnout is not a one-time journey but a continuous process of self-awareness and growth. As we navigate the ebb and flow of life, we must remember that it is not about being always "on", but about finding a balance that allows us to be productive without sacrificing our health and happiness. In this pursuit, understanding and setting boundaries becomes our greatest ally, helping us create a life of fulfillment, balance, and sustainability.

The exploration of boundaries and burnout reveals a profound truth: balance is not something we find, but something we create. By understanding the intricate interplay between boundaries and burnout, and actively shaping our lives to foster balance, we gain control over our well-being and, ultimately, our happiness. This journey may not be easy, and it may require us to confront uncomfortable truths about our habits and lifestyle. However, the rewards — a life lived with purpose, fulfillment, and sustainable energy — are well worth the effort.

What Is Burnout?

Burnout is a state of physical, emotional, and mental exhaustion caused by prolonged stress. The term was first coined by Herbert Freudenberger in 1974, and has since become widely recognized as a phenomenon that affects many people in today's fast-paced and demanding society (Maslach & Leiter, 2016). According to the World Health Organization (WHO), burnout is characterized by three main symptoms: feelings of energy depletion or exhaustion, increased mental distance from one's job, or feelings of negativism or cynicism related to one's job, and reduced professional efficacy.

Burnout is not a medical condition, but rather a response to chronic workplace stress. It can affect people in a variety of industries, including healthcare, education, and business. It can be caused by factors such as a lack of control over one's work, unrealistic expectations, and a lack of social support (Maslach & Leiter, 2016). It can also be brought on by a lack of balance between work and personal life, or a lack of recognition or rewards for hard work (WHO, 2019).

People who experience burnout may have difficulty sleeping, experience physical symptoms such as headaches and fatigue, and have a decreased ability to concentrate or make decisions (Maslach & Leiter, 2016). They may also experience emotional symptoms such as anxiety, depression, or feelings of hopelessness. Research has shown that burnout is a growing problem in today's society, with more and more people reporting symptoms of burnout.

According to a study by the American Institute of Stress (2019), 83% of US workers suffer from work-related stress, with 33% of those people reporting symptoms of burnout. Additionally, a study published in the Journal of Occupational Health Psychology found that burnout is not only a problem for individuals but also has a negative impact on organizations (Bakker, Demerouti, & Sanz-Vergel, 2014). The study found that burnout is linked to decreased job performance, increased absenteeism, and increased turnover rates.

It is important to recognize the signs of burnout and take steps to prevent it from happening. By prioritizing self-care, setting boundaries, seeking support, and practicing mindfulness, people can reduce their risk of experiencing burnout and improve their overall well-being.

Why Lack of Boundaries Can Lead to Burnout

Research has shown that a lack of boundaries can have serious consequences for our mental health and well-being. A study published in the Journal of Occupational Health Psychology found that employees who reported high levels of job demands and low levels of job control, two factors that can be related to a lack of boundaries, were more likely to experience symptoms of depression and anxiety. Another study published in the Journal of Health Psychology found that people who reported low levels of boundary management were more likely to report feeling overwhelmed and stressed. This research highlights the importance of setting clear boundaries to protect our mental health and well-being. By taking steps to manage our time and energy more effectively, we can reduce the risk of burnout and improve our overall quality of life.

Lack of boundaries can lead to burnout in several ways. When we fail to set clear limits on our time and energy, we can easily become overwhelmed and overworked. This can cause us to become exhausted, both physically and mentally, making it difficult to accomplish our goals and maintain a healthy work-life balance. One of the primary ways that lack of boundaries can contribute to burnout is by causing us to take on too many responsibilities at once. When we don't set limits on what we're willing to do, we can easily become overwhelmed by the sheer number of tasks and projects we have to manage. This can lead to feelings of stress and anxiety, as we struggle to keep up with everything that's been placed on our plate.

Consider this scenario: You're working on a project at work that you're passionate about. You want to do your best to ensure its success, so you begin taking on additional tasks and responsibilities. Before long, you're working long hours every day and even on weekends. You start feeling exhausted, both physically and mentally, and find it difficult to stay focused and motivated.

Your personal life starts to suffer too, as you don't have any time or energy left to spend with your family and friends.

In this scenario, a lack of boundaries has led to burnout. By not setting clear limits on your time and energy, you've taken on too much and are now struggling to keep up. This is a common trap that many of us fall into, especially when we're passionate about our work. However, it's important to recognize the signs of burnout and take steps to prevent it from happening in the first place. This might include setting clearer boundaries around your working hours and delegating tasks to others when possible. By taking these steps, you can avoid burnout and maintain a healthier work-life balance.

Understanding Stress and Burnout

Stress and burnout are two related concepts that are often used interchangeably, but they are not the same thing. Stress is a normal and natural response to certain situations or events, such as a deadline at work or a difficult conversation with a loved one. It is the body's way of reacting to a challenge or demand, and it can be beneficial in small doses as it can motivate and energize a person to take action. Stress is a common experience and it can be managed through a variety of coping mechanisms such as exercise, relaxation techniques, and seeking support from friends and family.

Burnout, on the other hand, is a state of chronic stress that has become overwhelming and debilitating for a person. It is characterized by feelings of emotional, mental and physical exhaustion, as well as a sense of detachment and loss of accomplishment. Unlike stress, burnout is not a normal response to stressors but rather a result of prolonged or chronic stress. It can have a negative impact on a person's overall well-being, and can lead to long-term negative effects on a person's physical and mental health, work performance, and personal relationships.

The causes of burnout can vary, but it is often related to a lack of control in a person's life, or a mismatch between a person's values and the demands of their job or personal life. It is also common among people who have a tendency to put the needs of others before their own, or who have a perfectionist attitude towards their work or personal life. For example, a person who is experiencing stress may have a deadline at work and feel pressure to complete a project on time. They may feel a sense of urgency and heightened alertness, which can motivate them to work efficiently and effectively. However, if the person is consistently under a high level of stress, it can lead to burnout. The person may begin to feel exhausted, detached from their work, and experience a loss of motivation and satisfaction. They may begin to feel overwhelmed, irritable, and may struggle to meet the demands of their job or personal life. In this example, stress is a normal and healthy response to the deadline, while burnout is a state of chronic stress that has become overwhelming and detrimental to the person's well-being.

Stress and burnout are related concepts, but they are not the same thing. Stress is a normal and healthy response to certain situations, while burnout is a state of chronic stress that can have negative effects on a person's overall well-being. By understanding the difference between stress and burnout, and implementing strategies for managing and preventing both, a person can improve their physical and mental well-being, and lead a more balanced and fulfilling life.

Exploring 3 Types of Burnout

Job burnout can be further broken down into three sub-types: overload burnout, under-challenged burnout, and neglect burnout, each with its own set of causes and symptoms.

Overload burnout is the most commonly recognized form of burnout and is caused by working at an unsustainable pace in pursuit of success, financial security, or recognition. People experiencing overload burnout may feel overwhelmed and exhausted by the constant demands of their job, leading to feelings of stress and anxiety. They may also experience physical symptoms such as headaches and fatigue, as well as emotional symptoms such as depression and feelings of hopelessness. For example, Sarah is a successful lawyer who has been working long hours for several months in order to meet a deadline for a big case. Despite her best efforts, she feels like she can never catch up on her work, and is constantly stressed and anxious. She has been experiencing frequent headaches and has trouble sleeping at night due to work-related worries.

Under-challenged burnout is caused by a lack of challenging work. People who experience this form of burnout may feel bored and disengaged in their job, leading to a lack of motivation and passion. They may also experience feelings of apathy and a sense of stagnation in their career, leading to a loss of interest and disconnection from their work. For example, Mike works in a call center, where he has to follow a script and handle the same types of customer complaints every day. He used to enjoy his job, but now finds it repetitive and boring. He has stopped caring about the quality of his work, and just goes through the motions in order to get through the day.

Neglect burnout is caused by a lack of purpose and agency at work. People who experience this form of burnout may feel helpless and disconnected from their job, leading to a sense of apathy and disengagement. They may also feel like their work is too complex or there is just too much to do, leading to a sense of overwhelm and burnout. This type of burnout can be particularly harmful for those who feel like nothing they do makes a difference, leading to a lack of motivation and engagement in their job. For example, John is a software engineer who has been working on a large project for the past year. Despite his hard work, he feels like his contributions are not valued by his team or his manager. He has lost faith in the project and no longer believes that it will make a difference in the world. He spends most of his time browsing the internet and has stopped engaging with his colleagues.

The Five Stages of Burnout

Research from Winona State University outlines the five stages of burnout, including the honeymoon phase, the balancing act, chronic stress symptoms, burnout, and enmeshment. These stages provide a roadmap for understanding the progression of burnout and the impact it can have on a person's mental and physical well-being.

The five stages of burnout, as outlined by research from Winona State University, are as follows:

The Honeymoon Phase: At the start of a new job or venture, people may feel excited and motivated by the work they are doing. They may feel a sense of creativity and energy, and may even put in extra hours without feeling fatigued. However, this positive outlook is often short-lived, and it's essential to maintain healthy habits in order to prolong this phase.

The Balancing Act: As the honeymoon phase ends, people may start to experience a mix of good and bad days at work. They may find that, while they can still maintain their performance, it is becoming increasingly taxing to do so. They may start to experience symptoms of stress, such as difficulty sleeping, forgetfulness, or an inability to relax. This stage is characterized by a sense of uncertainty as people try to balance their workload with their well-being.

Chronic Stress Symptoms: As stress persists, people may begin to feel uneasy and stressed more frequently. They may become resentful when asked to do additional work, and may feel exhausted, apathetic, or dependent on caffeine to get through the day. They may also experience depression, cynicism, and a sense of hopelessness. They may start to experience dread for the upcoming workweek.

Burnout: As the effects of stress continue to accumulate, people may start to experience the mental, emotional, and physical symptoms of burnout. They may start to avoid work, procrastinate, and miss deadlines. They may also start to contemplate quitting their job or running away from their situation. They may lose interest in their job, and may feel emotionally and physically drained.

Enmeshment: At this stage, burnout has become a person's default state. They may not be able to remember a time before they were experiencing burnout and may be diagnosed with anxiety or depression without recognizing burnout as the underlying cause. Burnout becomes a way of life, and the person may find it difficult to break free from the cycle of exhaustion and disengagement.

It's important to note that these stages are not linear, and not everyone will experience all of them, and people may jump back and forth between stages.

Signs You're Headed for Burnout

Those who experience burnout may not always attribute their symptoms to their job. Therefore, it is crucial to recognize the symptoms in order to know when to seek help and take appropriate action. To do so, familiarize yourself with the major signs of burnout listed below:

- **Constant fatigue and exhaustion** - You feel physically and mentally drained all the time, even after a full night's sleep.

- **Lack of motivation and engagement** - You find yourself procrastinating, disengaged, and uninspired in your work.

- **Increased stress and anxiety** - You feel anxious and stressed about work, even outside of work hours.

- **Difficulty concentrating** - You struggle to focus on work and find it hard to complete tasks.

- **Loss of interest in activities** - You no longer enjoy the activities and hobbies you used to love, and you have little energy for them.

- **Irritability and mood swings** - You find yourself easily frustrated, angry, or upset, even over small things.

- **Physical symptoms** - You experience physical symptoms such as headaches, back pain, or muscle tension.

- **Insomnia or difficulty sleeping** - You have trouble falling asleep or staying asleep, or you wake up feeling tired and unrefreshed.

- **Loss of appetite or overeating** - You find yourself either not eating or overeating, which can lead to weight loss or gain.

- **Increased absenteeism or lateness** - You find yourself taking more sick days or being late to work more frequently.

- **Difficulty making decisions or problem-solving** - You feel indecisive and struggle to make decisions or solve problems.

- **Social withdrawal or isolation** - You prefer to be alone and avoid social interactions, both at work and outside of work.

- **Feelings of hopelessness or helplessness** - You feel hopeless about your work and helpless to change your situation.

- **Decreased productivity or work quality** - You find that your work is not as productive as it used to be, and the quality of your work has decreased.

- **Lack of energy or enthusiasm** - You feel low energy, and you lack enthusiasm for your work and other activities.

- **Feeling overwhelmed or constantly bogged down** - You feel overwhelmed by the amount of work you have to do and the constant pressure to perform.

- **Negative self-talk or self-criticism** - You engage in negative self-talk or self-criticism, and you doubt your abilities and performance.

- **Difficulty separating work and personal life** - You have trouble disconnecting from work, and it often spills over into your personal life.

- **Feeling disconnected from work and colleagues** - You feel disconnected from your work and colleagues, and you feel no sense of fulfillment or satisfaction.

- **A decrease in overall well-being and happiness** - You feel a decrease in overall well-being and happiness, and you feel unfulfilled and unhappy in your work.

By being aware of these signs, you can take steps to prevent burnout and prioritize your mental health and well-being.

Exposing the Root Causes of Burnout

There are many reasons why people might experience burnout at work. Some of the most common reasons include:

1. Lack of control: When you feel like you have no control over your work environment, it can be very stressful. This might be because you are being asked to do more than you can handle, or because you are being micromanaged by a manager who doesn't trust you to do your job.

2. Lack of support: Feeling unsupported at work can be a major contributor to burnout. This might be because you don't feel like your colleagues or managers are helpful or because you feel like you are working in a toxic environment.

3. Lack of recognition: When you feel like your hard work and achievements are not being recognized, it can be very demoralizing. This can be especially true if you feel like you are not being given the opportunities or promotions you deserve.

4. Lack of work-life balance: Many of us struggle to find a balance between our work and personal lives. This can be especially difficult in today's fast-paced world, where technology allows us to be connected to our jobs 24/7.

5. Poor working conditions: Some of us experience burnout because we are working in environments that are not conducive to our well-being. This might be because we are working long hours, in unsafe conditions, or in a job that doesn't align with our values or interests.

6. Unfair treatment: This can include experiences of favouritism, mistreatment, misconduct, or bias, as well as unfair compensation or corporate policies. When you feel that you are being treated unfairly, it can lead to a lack of trust in your co-workers, supervisors, and leadership.

7. Overwhelming workload: When you have more work than you can reasonably handle, it can lead to poor performance and a lack of self-confidence on the job.

8. Lack of role clarity: If you are not clear on what is expected of you at work, or if those expectations keep changing, it can be exhausting and lead to confusion, uncertainty, and resentment.

9. Lack of communication and support: If you don't feel supported by your co-workers or if they are unable to address your concerns, it can leave you feeling isolated at work. If your co-workers are confrontational or neglectful, it can lead to feelings of burnout, defensiveness, and anger.

10. Unreasonable time pressure: Unrealistic deadlines or the perception that colleagues lack understanding of the effort required to execute a project or deliver outstanding customer service can result in daily stress and feelings of being overwhelmed, ultimately leading to burnout.

Burnout is a serious issue that can affect anyone, regardless of their profession or personal circumstances. The signs of burnout are diverse and may include physical and emotional exhaustion, decreased productivity, and a lack of motivation. It is important to recognize these signs early on and take steps to prevent burnout before it becomes a serious problem.

Exercise: Setting Boundaries and Burnout

1. Can you identify which of the three types of burnout you might be experiencing? At which stage of burnout do you think you are currently?
2. What are the signs that indicate you may be headed for burnout?
3. Have you ever experienced any of the five stages of burnout? If so, which stage(s)?
4. Can you recognize any root causes of burnout in your life?
5. How can setting boundaries help prevent or mitigate burnout?
6. What are some ways you can actively work on reducing burnout risk?
7. How do your current work boundaries contribute to or help prevent burnout?
8. Reflect on your current workload. Do you consistently feel overwhelmed or stressed? How can setting boundaries around your

workload potentially alleviate these feelings?

9.   Have you ever found yourself working outside of your designated work hours? If so, why did you choose to do so? What boundaries can you set to prevent this from happening?

10.   Are there specific situations or people at work that consistently drain your energy or cause stress? How could you establish boundaries in these situations to better protect your wellbeing?

11.   How do you respond to work-related communications outside of work hours? What boundaries could you put in place to ensure your personal time is respected?

12.   Have you ever felt obligated to take on a task or project that you knew would overload your capacity? How could boundary-setting have changed the outcome?

13.   Do you find it difficult to say "no" at work? How might practicing and enforcing the word "no" serve as a boundary and potentially prevent burnout?

14.   How much time do you spend on work-related tasks that could potentially be delegated or shared? Can setting boundaries around delegation help prevent burnout?

15.   Are you able to separate your self-worth from your work performance? If not, how might setting boundaries around your personal identity and work identity help?

16.   Reflect on a time when you felt close to burnout. What were the warning signs? How can you set boundaries in the future to avoid reaching this point again?

Chapter 3: Identifying Your Boundaries

"Boundaries are like fences around a yard. They keep the good in and the bad out."

– Jonathan Riley

Understanding the Power of Boundaries

Understanding the power of boundaries is the first step towards leading an authentic and balanced life. They are the guardians of our self-identity, the handmaids of our emotional health, and the architects of our personal freedom. Boundaries are more than just mental constructs; they are the lines that define our self-worth. They represent the power to decide for ourselves, to own our feelings, experiences, and, most importantly, our choices. They are the unseen but ever-present guardians who ensure we stay true to ourselves despite external pressures and expectations.

Just as countries assert their sovereignty through their borders, we as individuals express our autonomy through our personal boundaries. They are the tangible manifestations of our innermost values and needs, the physical expressions of our emotional landscape. Recognizing and respecting these boundaries are fundamental to our mental and emotional well-being. They remind us of our right to self-determination, empowering us to stand our ground, to seek respect, and to insist on being treated with dignity. A strong understanding of the power of boundaries leads to a profound shift in our perspective, allowing us to view ourselves not as passive recipients of other people's behaviors, but as active agents of our own lives.

Boundaries can be conceived of as invisible fences encircling our metaphorical yards of existence. They're our personal parameters, the guidelines we craft to protect our emotional, physical, and mental spaces, delineating what we find acceptable and what we deem intrusive. Just as a well-built fence secures a yard, keeping the desirable in and the undesirable out, so do our personal boundaries serve to cultivate a healthy internal environment, protecting us from negativity and harm.

Identifying your boundaries is akin to plotting the blueprint of your personal property. It's not about erecting impenetrable walls but rather setting the conditions for wholesome interactions and engagements. Boundaries help us strike a delicate balance amid the multitude of commitments that color our daily lives. They serve as our personal traffic signals, guiding when to speed up, slow down, stop, or yield, thereby preventing burnout and stress. They empower us to prioritize self-care, making space for the activities and relationships that truly nourish us.

Understanding your boundaries across various aspects of life - work, relationships, personal time - is a fundamental building block towards achieving a sense of balance, security, and fulfillment. It enables us to define who we are and what we value, to articulate our needs and desires with clarity and confidence. In the world of relationships, be it familial, platonic, or romantic, boundaries foster mutual respect and understanding, creating a safe space for genuine connection and growth.

The importance of boundaries cannot be overstated. They are not arbitrary or restrictive, but rather essential tools that facilitate authentic living. They allow us to preserve our integrity, to live in alignment with our values and aspirations. They protect our time and energy, ensuring we don't overextend ourselves or compromise our well-being. With well-established boundaries, we can say 'no' without guilt, 'yes' without resentment, and express our authentic feelings without fear of retribution or rejection.

Setting boundaries necessitates self-awareness and courage. It requires introspection to identify our needs, values, and limits, and strength to communicate and enforce them. However, the fruits of this labor are plentiful. Defined boundaries set the stage for personal growth, enabling us to pursue our passions and invest in meaningful relationships. They act as our personal compass, leading us towards a life that resonates with our true selves.

By setting necessary limits, we allow ourselves to flourish, nurturing our abilities, and cultivating deep, enriching relationships. They empower us to live on our own terms, to honor our individuality and celebrate our uniqueness. Boundaries are not just fences; they are the foundations of our self-respect, the borders of our personal freedom, and the custodians of our inner peace. In a world replete with demands and distractions, establishing our boundaries is a powerful act of self-love, a testament to our commitment to living a balanced, fulfilling, and authentic life.

Understanding Physical Boundaries

Physical boundaries refer to the limits we establish to protect our collective space, comfort, and well-being. They not only contribute to our mental and emotional health but also help prevent misunderstandings and conflicts among team members and clients. Setting physical boundaries can enhance productivity, improve communication, and create a more positive work environment. By clearly defining our shared space and comfort levels, we can focus on our tasks with minimal distractions and interruptions. Additionally, establishing physical boundaries can help maintain a professional atmosphere and protect us from harassment or unwanted advances.

Physical boundaries are of various types, each serving a unique purpose. These include personal space, touch, time, and property. Physical boundaries are the invisible lines that separate us and our personal space. They help maintain a sense of autonomy, safety, and privacy. These boundaries can be fluid and vary depending on factors such as culture, personal preferences, and situational context.

Personal space refers to the area immediately surrounding us that we consider as our private domain. This invisible buffer zone varies among us and depends on cultural norms, personal preferences, and the nature of the relationships within our environment. Touch is another essential component of physical boundaries, as it can convey various messages and emotions. Appropriate touch in the workplace is typically limited to a handshake, a pat on the back, or a brief touch on the arm. However, what is deemed appropriate may differ based on factors like culture, personal preferences, and comfort levels. Body language, including facial expressions, gestures, and posture, communicates unspoken messages and can indicate our physical boundaries. For example, crossed arms or leaning away from someone may signal that we are uncomfortable with the proximity or interaction. Environmental boundaries pertain to the physical layout and arrangement of the workspace, including considerations such as personal workstations, shared spaces, and the distance between colleagues. Respecting these boundaries can help promote privacy, minimize distractions, and create a comfortable working environment.

Establishing physical boundaries also safeguards us from harassment or unwanted advances. A professional atmosphere is one where everyone feels safe and respected. Physical boundaries help maintain this respect and protect us from uncomfortable or potentially harmful situations. Moreover, they serve as an effective tool for managing aggressive or overly friendly clients. By setting clear boundaries, we can ensure that our professional relationships remain just that - professional.

Managing physical boundaries, especially with aggressive or overly friendly clients, can be challenging, but it is necessary. It requires clarity, assertiveness, and respect for one's own rights and those of others. When a boundary is crossed, it's essential to communicate clearly and assertively, reminding the other party of the line of appropriateness that has been overstepped. By maintaining and enforcing these boundaries, we can ensure a respectful and productive professional relationship.

Physical boundaries help maintain a sense of autonomy, safety, and privacy. They serve as constant reminders of our individuality and independence, reminding us that while we are part of a team, we are also individuals deserving respect and dignity. They provide a sense of safety, ensuring that we can work comfortably without feeling threatened or violated. Moreover, they safeguard our privacy, keeping our personal and professional lives distinct and separate.

One example of effectively dealing with a situation where a coworker crossed physical boundaries is the story of Willow. Willow had always been an outgoing and friendly person, which made her a great fit for her role as a customer service representative at a busy tech company. She enjoyed her work environment and got along well with her colleagues. However, one day, a situation arose that tested her ability to maintain her physical boundaries at work.

A new employee, Mark, joined Willow's team, and from the very beginning, she noticed that he seemed to have a different understanding of personal space. During team meetings and casual conversations, Mark would consistently stand a little too close to Willow, making her feel uncomfortable. At first, Willow thought it was just a harmless quirk, but as time went on, she realized that Mark's behavior was crossing her personal boundaries.

Willow decided to take action and address the issue directly. She approached Mark during a break and asked if they could have a private conversation. In a calm and assertive manner, Willow explained to Mark how his behavior was making her uncomfortable. She told him that she valued their working relationship but would appreciate it if he could be more mindful of the physical space between them. Willow also mentioned that she understood different people had different comfort levels when it came to personal space, and she wanted to make sure they were on the same page.

Mark listened attentively and seemed genuinely surprised by Willow's concerns. He apologized and explained that he hadn't realized he was making her uncomfortable. Mark assured Willow that he would make a conscious effort to maintain a more appropriate distance in the future. Willow appreciated his understanding and willingness to adjust his behavior.

As the days went by, Willow noticed a significant improvement in Mark's behavior. He became more aware of his personal space and maintained a comfortable distance during their interactions. This positive change allowed Willow to feel more at ease and helped to strengthen their professional relationship.

In addition to addressing the issue with Mark, Willow also took the opportunity to reflect on her own personal boundaries and how she could maintain them more effectively. She realized the importance of paying attention to body language and nonverbal cues, both in herself and others.

Willow also recognized the value of open communication and being proactive in addressing any issues that arose concerning personal boundaries.

Willow's experience with Mark taught her the importance of setting and maintaining physical boundaries at work. By taking the initiative to address the issue directly, she was able to create a more comfortable working environment for herself and foster a healthier professional relationship with her co-worker. Furthermore, Willow's proactive approach to maintaining her personal boundaries served as a reminder to her colleagues of the significance of respecting each other's comfort levels and personal space in the workplace.

Physical boundaries are fundamental to a healthy and productive professional environment. By understanding their importance, types, and how to enforce them effectively, we can significantly improve our professional relationships, productivity, and overall work atmosphere. They are not barriers but bridges that help us connect with others in a respectful, meaningful, and effective way.

Navigating Mental Boundaries

Mental boundaries are the invisible lines you set for yourself in order to manage your thoughts, emotions, and actions. These boundaries are crucial for keeping a balance between work and your personal life, as well as for being productive and working well with others. By acknowledging the significance of mental boundaries and learning how to implement them, we can better navigate the challenges of our collective personal and professional lives, ultimately leading to a more satisfying and balanced life.

Mental boundaries denote the psychological limits we establish to safeguard our collective well-being and ward off burnout. These limits can cover various aspects of our lives, such as separating work and personal time, managing emotional responses, and communicating effectively with colleagues and managers. When mental boundaries are weak or non-existent, we may feel overwhelmed, exhausted, and disconnected from our work and personal lives.

The ability to disconnect from work during non-work hours is a crucial mental boundary. Studies have shown that when we successfully detach from work during our time off, we experience higher levels of job satisfaction, better physical health, and lower levels of fatigue, stress, and exhaustion. Conversely, if we fail to detach from work, we face increased stress and burnout. To establish this boundary, we may need to establish clear communication expectations, delegate tasks, and manage our collective time. For instance, we may choose to check emails only during specific hours of the day or decline phone calls outside of working hours. By setting these boundaries, we can better manage our workloads and reduce the risk of burnout.

Another key component of mental boundaries is managing emotions in a healthy and productive manner. This involves processing emotions effectively without letting them interfere with work. For instance, we might choose not to become angry or upset at work, opting instead to take time to process our emotions and develop a solution. By managing emotions healthily, we create a positive and productive work environment and can collaborate effectively with our colleagues.

Consider the case of Sloane, a dedicated marketing manager who recently felt overwhelmed and exhausted due to her demanding job. She constantly checked her emails even during her time off, which left her feeling drained. One day, Sarah decided to establish mental boundaries by ceasing to check her emails outside of work hours. She also delegated tasks to her team members and allocated time for self-care activities, such as exercise and meditation. As a result, Sloane was able to disconnect from work, focus on her personal life, and return to work feeling refreshed and energized.

Furthermore, Sloane set clear expectations for communication with her colleagues and supervisors by checking her emails only during specific times of the day and establishing boundaries around her availability for phone calls and meetings. This enabled her to manage her workload more effectively and reduced the risk of burnout. By setting these mental boundaries, Sloane not only became more productive and satisfied with her job but also had more time and energy for her personal life.

Mental boundaries are crucial for maintaining a healthy work-life balance, enhancing productivity, and fostering effective collaboration with others. By setting boundaries for disconnecting from work, communicating with colleagues and supervisors, and managing emotions, we are better equipped to cope with workplace demands and achieve our goals. Establishing and maintaining mental boundaries is essential for overall well-being and success in both our personal and professional lives.

Defining Emotional Boundaries

Emotional boundaries refer to the ways in which you set limits and manage your emotions in various aspects of life, particularly in the context of interpersonal relationships. These boundaries are essential for maintaining healthy relationships, both personal and professional, and promoting a positive environment in different spheres of life, including the workplace. Emotional boundaries can be understood as the ability to separate personal and professional emotions when interacting with others, especially when making decisions or dealing with work-related issues. While emotions and personal connections with colleagues are natural, it is crucial to be able to set those aside when needed. This means being able to disagree with a colleague or provide constructive criticism without taking it personally or becoming emotionally invested in the outcome.

Having emotional boundaries means being able to control and regulate your emotions rather than allowing them to control or dictate behavior. This includes not allowing anger or frustration to dictate how you interact with colleagues or handle a difficult situation, and not allowing sadness or stress to negatively impact your ability to perform your job. Emotional boundaries are also vital in preventing emotional contagion, a phenomenon where emotions spread among individuals, which can significantly affect the overall productivity and well-being of the workplace (Kokkoris & Keltner, 2020).

Communication is key when it comes to setting and maintaining emotional boundaries. It is important to be able to express your own needs and boundaries clearly and assertively, while also being able to actively listen and understand the needs and boundaries of others. This means being able to have honest and open conversations about emotions and setting boundaries when necessary, which can help maintain a healthy work-life balance and create a more positive work environment for everyone involved.

Imagine you are a project manager working on an important project with a tight deadline. You have been working closely with a colleague, Carter, who is responsible for a critical component of the project. However, Carter has been underperforming and has missed several deadlines, putting the entire project at risk. You are frustrated and angry with Carter and feel like her lack of effort is personally affecting you and your work. However, you recognize that it is crucial to set emotional boundaries and avoid letting your emotions affect your behavior or communication with Carter.

You decide to have a conversation with Carter and express your concerns about her performance in a calm and professional manner, without letting your emotions get the best of you. You make it clear that her delays are affecting the project and provide her with specific examples of missed deadlines and incomplete work. You also offer your support and assistance to help her meet the project's expectations.

By maintaining emotional boundaries, you avoid letting your anger or frustration dictate your behavior and communication with Carter. Instead, you communicate effectively and assertively, while still being supportive and empathetic. This approach allows you to address the issue at hand while maintaining a positive and respectful working relationship with Carter.

A study by the American Psychological Association found that employees who had poor emotional boundaries were more likely to experience burnout and job dissatisfaction, leading to higher levels of absenteeism and turnover (APA, 2021). Furthermore, the study discovered that setting emotional boundaries can improve job performance by lowering the likelihood of emotional contagion, which occurs when negative emotions spread among colleagues and impact overall productivity (Kokkoris & Keltner, 2020).

Emotional boundaries play a significant role in ensuring a healthy work-life balance and fostering a positive work environment for everyone. By understanding the importance of setting limits and managing emotions, we can effectively navigate the challenges that come with personal and professional relationships, ultimately leading to improved job satisfaction and performance. By implementing emotional boundaries, we can cultivate a supportive and empathetic atmosphere, which is conducive to increased productivity and overall well-being.

Exploring Internal Boundaries

Internal boundaries, unique to each individual, are established with oneself to set limits on personal behavior and actions, safeguarding one's physical and emotional well-being. This can be a challenging endeavor, as we frequently strive to achieve more, but it is essential for maintaining a healthy, balanced life. One key aspect to consider when setting internal boundaries is recognizing your own physical and emotional limitations.

In order to effectively establish these boundaries, it's crucial to pay attention to your body and mind, taking care of yourself when you're tired, stressed, or overwhelmed. This might require limiting your workload or taking time to rest and relax when necessary. For instance, if you consistently work late into the night, you might need to set a boundary to stop working at a certain hour, ensuring you get enough sleep for optimal functioning the next day. Similarly, if you're constantly accepting social invitations when feeling burnt out, it may be beneficial to set a boundary for declining some commitments, allowing time for self-care.

By setting internal boundaries, you protect your time and energy, limiting the amount of time spent on specific activities and declining commitments misaligned with your values or goals. It's equally important to allocate time for yourself and your interests, rather than always prioritizing others' needs. This involves setting boundaries with those who may consume too much of your time and ensuring you have time for activities that bring joy and fulfillment. Remember that it's perfectly acceptable to prioritize your own needs and say no when necessary.

An integral part of setting personal boundaries is placing limits on your own behavior and being honest with yourself about your needs and desires. This means being truthful about your true aspirations, rather than merely conforming to others' expectations, and acknowledging your own limitations without trying to be someone you're not. For example, if you struggle to wake up early and you're not a morning person, it's important to be honest with yourself and set a boundary for waking up at a suitable time. Keep in mind that setting personal boundaries requires practice, and it's perfectly fine to re-evaluate and adjust them as needed. Setting internal boundaries is not about selfishness or erecting barriers; rather, it's about self-care and giving to others from a place of abundance instead of depletion.

Consider London, a young professional who recently began working at a marketing firm. Eager to make a good impression, she often takes on more work than she can handle, working long hours and frequently bringing work home. Despite her exhaustion, she feels guilty for not responding to work emails outside of work hours. Eventually, London recognizes that her workload has become unmanageable, and she's neglecting her own well-being. Realizing the need for self-imposed boundaries, she takes action to maintain her physical and emotional health.

London sets a boundary to cease working after a specific time in the evening and disconnect her work phone after hours. She also limits the number of projects she accepts and prioritizes her tasks based on importance. After informing her colleagues and clients of her new boundaries, they respect her decision. Consequently, London gains control over her workload and life, enjoying better sleep, pursuing her hobbies, and feeling more fulfilled outside of work. She also becomes more productive at work, effectively managing her time and responsibilities. By setting personal boundaries, London leads a healthier, more balanced life.

Setting internal boundaries is a vital aspect of self-care and personal development. This process involves being honest with yourself about your own needs and desires, and setting limits on your behavior and actions to protect your physical and emotional well-being. Through establishing personal boundaries, you can lead a healthier, happier, and more balanced life. Remember that this is an ongoing process, and it's crucial to be patient and kind to yourself throughout the journey.

The Importance of Time Boundaries

Effective time management is essential for achieving our personal and professional goals. One critical aspect of managing time is establishing time boundaries, which serve as protective measures for our time and energy from outside demands and distractions. Time boundaries are limits that we set to help manage our time effectively, ensuring that we dedicate our time to essential tasks and activities that align with our goals and values. These boundaries also prevent the encroachment of others on our time and protect against becoming overwhelmed by demands on our time.

Without clear boundaries, it can be easy for others to take advantage of your time, leading you to work long hours, neglect other areas of your life, and ultimately become burnt out. Setting boundaries also helps to ensure that you're spending your time on the things that are most important to you, rather than getting bogged down by less important tasks or distractions. Research has shown that people who establish time boundaries are more likely to experience increased productivity, reduced stress, and improved work-life balance (Kelly & Moen, 2007).

There are several strategies you can use to set boundaries in your life in order to better manage your time. One approach is to set specific time limits for different tasks or activities. For example, you might decide to only check your email at certain times of the day, rather than constantly throughout the day, as research has shown that constantly checking email can be detrimental to productivity (Kushlev & Dunn, 2015). Another strategy is to set limits on the amount of time you spend on certain activities, such as social media or TV, as excessive use of these activities has been linked to negative outcomes such as decreased well-being and poorer sleep quality (Woods & Scott, 2016).Jane is a freelance graphic designer who works from home. She has multiple clients who send her design projects to complete within a certain timeframe. However, Jane often finds herself getting distracted by social media notifications, household chores, and personal phone calls, which eats into her work time. She also feels guilty saying "no" to her clients when they send urgent requests outside of her agreed-upon schedule, which causes her to work long hours and miss out on important family time.

To address these issues, Jane decides to set clear boundaries for her work time. She schedules specific blocks of time for work and designates a quiet, distraction-free workspace in her home. She also sets clear expectations with her clients about her work hours and communicates that she will only take on urgent projects outside of her agreed-upon schedule in exceptional circumstances. By setting these boundaries, Jane is able to manage her time more effectively and be more productive during work hours. She also feels less stressed and guilty about taking personal time for herself and her family, knowing that she has communicated her work boundaries clearly to her clients. Overall, Jane's work and personal life are more balanced and fulfilling as a result of setting boundaries in her time management.

By creating psychological boundaries, you can learn to distinguish between work time and leisure time and focus on what needs to be done during work hours and enjoy yourself during your leisure hours. Learning to say "no" is another important step in setting boundaries. It's easy to get caught up in the demands of others and to take on more tasks than you can handle. By learning to say "no" to requests or demands that don't align with your goals or values, you can free up time and energy for the things that are most important to you. Setting clear limits on the demands on your time, protecting your time and energy, and learning to say "no" are all important aspects of effective time management. By doing so, you can better manage your time and achieve your goals. Remember to be mindful of your time and energy and to be intentional in how you spend it.

Establishing and maintaining time boundaries is a key factor in effective time management, leading to increased productivity, reduced stress, and improved work-life balance. By setting specific time limits, communicating your boundaries clearly, learning to say "no," periodically reviewing and adjusting your boundaries, practicing self-compassion, and balancing between maintaining boundaries and being flexible, you can achieve your personal and professional goals while enjoying a fulfilling and balanced life.

Exploring Relationship Boundaries

Relationship boundaries refer to how you interact with your colleagues and supervisors. It is essential to treat everyone with respect and kindness, regardless of their position or status in the company. This includes refraining from engaging in gossip or negative talk about your colleagues and avoiding making assumptions or stereotypes about others. Furthermore, it is important to be aware of power dynamics within the workplace and avoid taking advantage of or exploiting your colleagues or supervisors. To establish personal and professional boundaries, it is necessary to separate personal and professional relationships. Mixing the two can lead to conflicts and misunderstandings. This includes avoiding sharing personal details with your colleagues or supervisors and not getting involved in personal issues that do not relate directly to work.

Let's meet Emily. Emily is a new employee at a company and is excited to start working with her team. She quickly becomes friendly with her supervisor, Sarah, and they begin to share personal stories and experiences. Emily feels comfortable discussing her personal life with Sarah, but soon realizes that Sarah is sharing this information with other colleagues during team meetings. Emily begins to feel uncomfortable and exposed, as she did not give permission for this information to be shared. Emily's work performance begins to suffer as she becomes distracted and loses trust in her supervisor.

In this scenario, Sarah violated Emily's personal and professional boundaries by sharing her personal information without her consent. This situation could have been avoided if Sarah had established clear relationship boundaries with Emily and respected her personal privacy. It is crucial for supervisors and colleagues to separate personal and professional relationships to prevent conflicts and misunderstandings.

According to a study in the Journal of Applied Psychology, open communication among coworkers was associated with higher job satisfaction and a lower risk of burnout (Halbesleben & Buckley, 2004). According to this research, direct and open communication can promote good relationships and avoid miscommunications and conflicts at work. In addition, a Harvard Business Review study discovered that workers who felt respected by their coworkers reported higher levels of wellbeing and lower levels of burnout (O'Neill & Emmons, 2019). These findings emphasize the value of treating others with respect in order to promote fruitful working relationships and a productive workplace.

Research supports the importance of setting relationship boundaries for creating a productive, respectful, and healthy work environment. Respecting personal space and privacy, effective communication, and treating colleagues with respect and kindness are all essential components of maintaining healthy work relationships. By establishing clear expectations and boundaries, employees can work together effectively and create a positive work environment for all.

Understanding Task Boundaries

In order to complete your tasks effectively and efficiently, it is crucial to establish task boundaries with work. The distinct divisions between the various tasks or responsibilities you have are referred to as task boundaries. These boundaries can be physical, such as having a separate workspace for each task, or they can be psychological, such as having clear expectations and guidelines for each task you undertake.

Clear task boundaries are essential for a variety of reasons. Firstly, it helps to prevent task interference, which occurs when one task interferes with the completion of another task. This can happen when you are not clear on what your specific responsibilities are for a certain task, and as a result, you may become overwhelmed and unable to complete the task efficiently. Secondly, clear task boundaries can help to increase motivation and job satisfaction. When you have a clear understanding of what is expected of you, you are more likely to feel a sense of purpose and accomplishment in your work. This can lead to increased motivation and engagement, which can ultimately lead to better performance and productivity. Thirdly, having clear task boundaries can help to promote a sense of organisation and structure in your work. When you are aware of your specific roles and responsibilities, you are more likely to prioritise and manage your time more effectively. This can lead to improved productivity, and help you achieve your goals more efficiently.

Meet Everly, a marketing manager for a software company. Everly is responsible for a variety of tasks, including managing social media accounts, creating marketing materials, and organizing events. She often finds herself struggling to stay focused and productive, as her various responsibilities tend to overlap and interfere with one another. One day, Everly decides to establish clear task boundaries to improve her work performance. She creates a separate workspace for each task, ensuring that she can focus solely on the task at hand without distractions. She also creates a to-do list with specific deadlines and deliverables for each task, helping her prioritize and manage her time effectively.

Thanks to her clear task boundaries, Everly notices a significant improvement in her work performance. She no longer feels overwhelmed or stressed, as she knows exactly what is expected of her for each task. She completes each task more efficiently, preventing task interference and ensuring that all tasks are completed on time. Everly also experiences a boost in motivation and job satisfaction. With a clear understanding of what is expected of her, she feels a sense of purpose and accomplishment in her work, leading to increased engagement and productivity. She is also able to better organize her work, leading to improved productivity and efficient goal achievement. By establishing and maintaining clear task boundaries, Everly has become more effective and efficient in her work. She has improved her performance, productivity, and overall success in achieving her goals.

According to a study in the Journal of Occupational Health Psychology, employees' job performance and job satisfaction were both positively correlated with clearly defined task boundaries. According to the study, those with clearly defined task boundaries felt more engaged in their work and were more productive than those without such boundaries. The study found that workers who had defined task boundaries reported higher job satisfaction and higher levels of engagement.

Overall, these studies suggest that establishing clear task boundaries can have positive effects on job satisfaction, job performance, and productivity. By providing clear guidelines and expectations for each task, employees are more likely to feel engaged, motivated, and organized in their work, leading to improved performance and success in achieving their goals.

Setting Boundaries Around Personal Information

Maintaining boundaries around personal information is crucial to safeguard your privacy and prevent any potential conflicts or misunderstandings. While it may be tempting to share personal details with your colleagues, such as your financial situation, family issues, health information, or personal beliefs, it's important to consider the potential implications of doing so.

Sharing financial information may lead to questions or even judgment from others, while discussing personal beliefs may create conflicts or tension. Moreover, personal information shared can quickly spread beyond the intended audience, ending up in the hands of those who should not have it. Therefore, it's important to be cautious and mindful of the information you share and with whom you share it.

Remember that you have the right to privacy regarding certain personal information, and you're under no obligation to share anything with your colleagues that you're not comfortable disclosing. It's vital to establish your own boundaries and communicate them clearly to others. You can set limits on what information you're willing to share and make it clear that certain topics are off-limits for discussion. If you feel uncomfortable or pressured to share personal information, don't hesitate to speak up and let others know that you're not comfortable sharing that information. Ultimately, you're in control of your own personal information, and you have the right to keep it private if you choose to do so.

Meet Jane, a new employee at a marketing agency. On her first day, Jane introduces herself to her team and shares a bit about her personal life, including her passion for running marathons and her recent breakup with her boyfriend. She thinks that by sharing these personal details, she can build connections and relationships with her colleagues. However, as the week progresses, Jane begins to feel uneasy as her colleagues ask her more personal questions and pry into her life. Some colleagues ask her about her financial situation, while others ask her for relationship advice or her opinion on personal beliefs. Jane feels uncomfortable sharing such intimate details about her life and worries that her colleagues may judge her or gossip behind her back.

In this scenario, it's essential for Jane to recognize that she has the right to set her own boundaries around personal information. While it's natural to want to build connections and relationships with colleagues, oversharing personal information can lead to misunderstandings and conflicts. By communicating her boundaries clearly and respectfully, Jane can maintain her privacy and protect herself from unwanted scrutiny. For example, Jane could politely decline to answer personal questions and steer the conversation towards a different topic. She could also let her colleagues know that while she's happy to socialize and get to know everyone, there are some personal details that she's not comfortable sharing at work. By doing so, Jane can establish a culture of respect and professionalism that values privacy and mutual respect.

According to a study published in the Journal of Business and Psychology, employees who reveal personal information are more likely to experience emotional exhaustion and burnout. Employees who set personal information sharing boundaries, according to the study, can better manage their emotional resources and reduce burnout. (Bock, 2017).

Maintaining boundaries around personal information is essential for protecting your privacy and avoiding potential conflicts. By being mindful of what you share and respecting others' boundaries, you can establish a safe and respectful workplace culture that values privacy and mutual respect.

The Importance of Communication Boundaries

Communication boundaries refer to the rules and guidelines that you establish to govern the exchange of information and ideas in a professional setting. Communication boundaries are important because they help colleagues establish a sense of respect and professionalism. When you are clear about what you expect from others in terms of communication, you are more likely to treat them with respect and to avoid engaging in behavior that may be perceived as rude or inappropriate. For example, setting boundaries around the use of profanity or personal attacks can help to create a more positive and professional work environment for you and your colleagues. The benefit of communication boundaries is that they promote effective communication. When you understand the communication boundaries, you are more likely to communicate in a clear, direct, and to-the-point manner. This can help to avoid confusion, misunderstandings, and delays in getting things done. You are less likely to share sensitive or confidential information that could be harmful to yourself or others if you understand what is and is not appropriate to communicate.

When you understand what is and is not acceptable in terms of communication, you are less likely to engage in behavior that may be perceived as harassing or abusive. This can help to create a culture of respect and trust, which can be essential for building strong relationships and achieving organisational goals. Setting boundaries for communication helps to establish a sense of respect and professionalism among coworkers, which in turn facilitates more effective communication.

Let's meet Samantha who is a new employee at a marketing agency, and she's excited to start her new job. However, she notices that some of her coworkers tend to interrupt her when she's speaking, or talk over her in meetings. While she tries to speak up and assert herself, she's finding it difficult to get her ideas heard. After a few weeks of feeling frustrated and unheard, Samantha decides to set a communication boundary by requesting that her coworkers allow her to finish speaking before they respond or interrupt. She also asks them to avoid talking over her during meetings.

Initially, some of her coworkers are resistant to this boundary, as they're used to having more assertive conversations. However, Samantha is firm but polite in her request, and explains that it's important for her to be heard and feel valued as a team member. Her coworkers eventually come to respect her boundary, and they start to give her the time and space she needs to share her ideas effectively. By setting this communication boundary, Samantha is able to establish a sense of respect and professionalism with her coworkers. She's also promoting effective communication by ensuring that everyone has a chance to speak and be heard, which can lead to better collaboration and stronger outcomes for the team.

According to a study published in the Journal of Applied Psychology, setting communication boundaries is associated with higher job satisfaction and lower work-family conflict among employees. The study also discovered that employees who established clear communication boundaries reported greater feelings of control over their work and personal lives. (Shockley, Shen, DeNunzio, & Arvan, 2017). These findings suggest that communication boundaries are an important factor in creating a positive and productive work environment.

By setting clear boundaries around communication, you can help to create a positive work environment that is respectful, safe, and supportive. It is important to understand the importance of communication boundaries, and to establish appropriate boundaries that will help to foster a healthy and productive work environment for you and your colleagues.

Self-Assessment - Identifying Your Boundaries

Understanding and respecting boundaries, both our own and those of others, is essential for creating a healthy, productive, and respectful workplace. This self-assessment is designed to help you introspect on your understanding and practice of boundaries in your professional life. It covers various aspects from physical to emotional, and from time to relationship boundaries. By evaluating your responses, you will gain insight into your strengths and areas where you might need to focus more. Remember, there is no right or wrong answer; this is an exercise in self-awareness and personal growth.

For each question, answer with "Yes" or "No."

1. Are you aware of the physical boundaries that are important to you in the workplace (e.g., personal space, a comfortable work environment)?

2. Do you effectively maintain mental boundaries at work by focusing on your tasks and avoiding unnecessary distractions?
3. Are you able to protect your emotional well-being in the workplace by not taking things personally and managing your emotions?
4. Have you established internal boundaries that guide your behavior and decision-making?
5. Do you set clear time boundaries to ensure you allocate sufficient time for both work and personal life?
6. Do you maintain healthy relationship boundaries with your colleagues and supervisors by maintaining professionalism and respecting their boundaries?
7. Have you set task boundaries that help you prioritize your workload and avoid taking on too many responsibilities?
8. Are you careful about sharing personal information in the workplace and know what information is appropriate to share?
9. Do you maintain communication boundaries by being respectful and assertive in your interactions with co-workers and supervisors?
10. Are you confident in asserting and maintaining your boundaries when faced with challenges in the workplace?
11. Can you recognize when your boundaries are being violated and take appropriate action?
12. Do you seek a balance between being flexible and maintaining your boundaries when faced with changing circumstances?
13. Do you consistently evaluate and adjust your boundaries based on your personal and professional growth?
14. Do you understand the importance of setting boundaries for your mental and emotional well-being?
15. Are you open to feedback and willing to adjust your boundaries if they are negatively impacting your work relationships?
16. Are you able to say "no" when necessary to maintain your boundaries in the workplace?
17. Do you maintain a healthy balance between setting boundaries and collaborating effectively with your team?
18. Do you recognize that setting and maintaining boundaries is an ongoing process and commit to continually refining your

approach?

After answering all the questions, count the number of "Yes" responses. A higher number of "Yes" responses indicates a stronger understanding and practice of setting boundaries. Use your results to identify areas where you can improve your boundary-setting skills and create a healthier work environment.

Remember that boundary setting is a dynamic process that evolves with our personal and professional growth. The areas where you answered "No" are opportunities for learning and improvement. Consider these points as you continue your journey towards creating a healthier work environment, improving your relationships, and ensuring your mental and emotional well-being. Remember, maintaining effective boundaries is a sign of self-respect and respect for others. Keep evaluating, refining, and growing.

Exercise: Identifying Your Boundaries

1. How have you seen a lack of boundaries impacting your productivity or satisfaction at work? What actions can you take to establish stronger boundaries?
2. Reflect on your physical workspace. Is it conducive to your productivity and well-being? What physical boundaries could you set or adjust to improve your work environment?
3. Are there thoughts or worries that you often bring home from work? How could setting mental boundaries help you leave work-related stress at the office?
4. How do you react when people infringe upon your emotional boundaries? How can you assert these boundaries more effectively?
5. How does your self-talk influence your boundaries at work? Are there ways you can adjust your internal dialogue to better support your boundary setting?
6. How often do you find yourself working beyond your designated work hours? What changes can you make to respect your time boundaries more consistently?
7. Reflect on your relationships at work. Are there any relationships

that could benefit from clearer boundaries? What steps can you take to establish these boundaries?

8. Have you ever found yourself overwhelmed by tasks that are not part of your job description? How can you communicate and enforce your task boundaries more effectively?

9. How comfortable are you with sharing personal information at work? Are there any areas where you feel you need to set stronger boundaries?

10. What steps can you take to ensure that your boundaries are not just set, but also respected by others? How can you better respect the boundaries of your colleagues?

11. Are there any people with whom you feel you need to set stronger boundaries? What specific changes could you make to improve these relationships?

12. Reflect on a time when a co-worker overstepped a boundary. How did you handle it, and how might you handle a similar situation differently in the future?

13. Have you ever felt your personal life was being encroached upon by work-related matters due to other people's actions? What boundaries could you set to ensure work-life balance?

14. Are there any situations where you feel others cross boundaries in terms of personal space or personal matters? How can you address this to ensure a comfortable working environment?

15. How often do you feel pressured to respond to work communications (emails, calls, messages) outside of your working hours by managers? What steps can you take to establish clearer communication boundaries?

16. If a manager consistently assigns you tasks that are not within your job description or professional capacity, how can you respectfully communicate and enforce your task boundaries?

Chapter 4: Assessing Your Current Work-Life Balance

"Work-life balance is not about dividing your time evenly, it's about dividing your priorities." – Brian Dyson

Evaluating Your Work-Life Balance

As we navigate the labyrinth of life, finding equilibrium between our professional and personal lives has become increasingly challenging. This delicate dance, often referred to as "work-life balance," is not merely about dividing your time evenly. Rather, it's about dividing your priorities, carving out the space and time necessary for both the professional and personal aspects of your life to thrive. In our modern society, where the boundaries between work and home have become blurred, understanding the importance of this balance and how to evaluate it is paramount.

Work-life balance is not a one-size-fits-all formula. It is a delicate, ever-shifting balance that requires constant self-evaluation and adjustment. Some key indicators of imbalance might be feeling perpetually tired, being unable to disconnect from work, or neglecting personal relationships or hobbies. These symptoms may seem manageable at first, but left unaddressed, they can lead to burnout and negatively impact our physical, emotional, and mental health.

Work-related stressors are often the hidden culprits contributing to an unbalanced lifestyle. The pressure to meet deadlines, maintain quality standards, and keep up with the pace of technological advancements can erode the boundaries we set between our personal and professional lives. Furthermore, the advent of remote work and the constant accessibility provided by technology can make it difficult to "switch off," leading to an unhealthy merging of work and personal time.

One particular phenomenon tied to this is productivity guilt, the nagging feeling that we should be doing more, working harder, being constantly productive. Overcoming productivity guilt is essential to achieving work-life balance. It involves understanding that our worth is not solely tied to our output and that rest, relaxation, and personal fulfillment are equally important aspects of a well-rounded life.

Setting boundaries can be a crucial tool in mitigating the pressure to be constantly productive. By clearly delineating when we are "on the clock" and when we are not, we can better focus our energies on what truly matters at any given moment. This could mean shutting off work-related notifications after a certain time, designating specific work-free zones in our homes, or even dedicating specific hours to uninterrupted personal time.

Despite their benefits, many people are hesitant to set boundaries. This hesitation often stems from fear – fear of appearing uncommitted, fear of missing out, fear of disappointing others. Yet, it's important to remember that setting boundaries isn't about being selfish; it's about self-preservation. It's about ensuring that we have the energy, focus, and emotional capacity to perform at our best in every area of our lives.

The quest for work-life balance is not a destination but a journey, one that requires constant self-awareness and evaluation. It is about identifying and managing work-related stressors, overcoming productivity guilt, and setting boundaries to ensure that we can focus on what truly matters. It's about understanding that it's not just about how much we work, but how well we live. By nurturing self-care and setting clear boundaries, we can navigate the challenging terrain of work-life balance, cultivating a life of productivity and fulfillment in all its dimensions.

Why We Avoid Setting Boundaries

In today's achievement-oriented society, many of us grapple with establishing clear boundaries between our personal and professional lives. This struggle can lead to work-life imbalance, adversely affecting our mental and physical well-being. There are several factors that contribute to this difficulty in setting boundaries, and understanding them can help us take the necessary steps to achieve a healthier work-life balance.

One primary reason we find it challenging to set boundaries is the strong desire to please our employers or colleagues. This need to appease others often stems from a fear of disappointment or a belief that our self-worth is intrinsically tied to our productivity and achievements at work. According to a study published in the Journal of Occupational and Environmental Medicine, excessive workloads and long working hours can result in negative consequences for us, such as increased stress, depression, and sleep disturbances (Dembe et al., 2005). Another significant factor contributing to the difficulty in setting boundaries is the constant advancement of technology. With the ubiquity of email, messaging apps, and other communication tools, we are often expected to be accessible around the clock. This "always-on" work culture can blur the lines between personal and professional lives, making it increasingly challenging for us to establish boundaries and maintain a healthy work-life balance. In fact, research conducted by the American Psychological Association found that constant connectivity to work can lead to increased stress levels, anxiety, and burnout (American Psychological Association, 2017).

Moreover, some of us might not set boundaries due to a lack of awareness about the negative impacts of overworking. For these people, overworking may be perceived as a badge of honour or a testament to their commitment to their job. However, several studies have shown that overworking can lead to burnout, higher stress levels, and a decline in overall well-being (Virtanen et al., 2012). Tragically, many of us fail to acknowledge these negative consequences until it's too late.

Lastly, fear of the consequences of saying no or pushing back against employer expectations can hinder us from setting boundaries. This fear might originate from concerns about job loss or damaging our professional reputation. Consequently, some of us may continue to take on excessive work or work beyond our usual hours, even if it is not sustainable long-term.

The failure to set boundaries with work can have significant adverse effects on our well-being and work-life balance. While numerous reasons contribute to the struggle in establishing boundaries, it is crucial to recognize that setting limits is essential for maintaining a healthy and fulfilling life. By prioritizing self-care, communicating clearly with employers and colleagues, and learning to say no, we can establish healthy boundaries and create a more sustainable work-life balance.

The Complex Drivers of Overworking

Overworking has emerged as a pervasive issue in contemporary society, compelling many of us to work longer and harder than ever before. This phenomenon stems from a complex interplay of economic, social, and psychological factors. Various elements contribute to overworking and the profound implications it holds for both us and society at large.

Economic pressures are among the most notable drivers of overworking. The expansion of the gig economy and escalating job competition have pushed many of us to extend our working hours simply to make ends meet. This predicament is particularly challenging for those already grappling with income inequality (Kalleberg, 2018). Moreover, advances in technology and the ubiquity of social media have facilitated employer-employee communication beyond regular working hours, fostering an expectation of constant availability (Mazmanian, Orlikowski & Yates, 2013).

Societal expectations and cultural norms also fuel the drive to overwork. In numerous cultures, hard work is perceived as the cornerstone of success, and those who do not work diligently enough are deemed uncommitted to their jobs (Hofstede, 2001). Such a mindset can lead us to push ourselves beyond our limits, working harder and longer than is healthy or sustainable. The emergence of "hustle culture" further exacerbates this issue, pressuring many of us to relentlessly pursue our next goal or project (Gershon, 2019).

Psychological factors likewise contribute to overworking. Perfectionism and fear of failure can prompt us to work to excess, striving to ensure our output is of the highest caliber (Stoeber & Rennert, 2008). Burnout and work-related stress can also instigate overworking, as we feel compelled to extend our hours to meet deadlines or manage mounting workloads (Maslach, Schaufeli & Leiter, 2001). Furthermore, low self-esteem and the desire for validation can drive us to work harder as a means of proving our worth (Orth, Robins & Meier, 2009).

The repercussions of overworking are significant and wide-ranging. On a physical level, overworking can result in fatigue, insomnia, and a myriad of other health issues (Sparks et al., 1997). Mentally, it can exacerbate depression, anxiety, and other mental health disorders (Frone, 2000). Overworking can also strain relationships and family life, as we lack the time and energy to dedicate to our loved ones (Pleck, 1997). Additionally, overworking can diminish productivity and job performance, as exhaustion and burnout take their toll (Demerouti et al., 2001).

It is crucial to acknowledge that overworking should not be considered a badge of honor or be glorified. Instead, we must shift our cultural and societal paradigms to appreciate rest and balance as much as hard work. This involves celebrating those who prioritize their well-being and acknowledging the vital role of rest and relaxation in achieving success (Nippert-Eng, 1996). Overworking has serious consequences, affecting our physical and mental health, personal relationships, and job performance. By understanding the complex drivers behind overworking, we can work towards fostering a more balanced and sustainable approach to work and life.

Overcoming Productivity Guilt

Productivity guilt is a feeling of guilt or inadequacy that can arise when we feel we are not being productive enough. This phenomenon is often associated with the belief that we should always be working or achieving goals, leading to feelings of stress and anxiety. We who are prone to productivity guilt may feel guilty for taking breaks, relaxing, or not working on a task, even when it is necessary for our well-being (Barker, 2016). Research suggests that productivity guilt can arise from societal pressure to be productive, perfectionism, and an unhealthy work-life balance (Leiter & Maslach, 2000).

Boundaries and productivity guilt are two concepts that are closely related and can have a significant impact on our lives and work. Setting boundaries is essential for maintaining a healthy work-life balance and increasing productivity, while productivity guilt can make us feel overwhelmed, stressed, and guilty for not achieving more (Leiter & Maslach, 2000).

A study published in the Journal of Occupational Health Psychology found that people who experience high levels of productivity guilt are more likely to report symptoms of burnout and depression and are less likely to engage in self-care behaviors such as exercise and relaxation (Leiter & Maslach, 2000). Perfectionism is a common factor that can contribute to productivity guilt. The study also discovered that people with high levels of perfectionism were more likely to experience feelings of guilt and shame when they failed to meet their own high standards (Stoeber & Otto, 2006).

Olivia, a 32-year-old marketing executive, had been struggling with productivity guilt for years. She often found herself working late into the night and on weekends, believing that if she wasn't constantly working, she was wasting time. Olivia's productivity guilt stemmed from societal pressure to be successful and her own perfectionism. Despite her long hours, she felt she was never doing enough and had difficulty enjoying her downtime without feeling guilty.

The impact of productivity guilt on Olivia's life was significant. Her relationships suffered, her health declined, and she experienced symptoms of burnout and depression. She had stopped engaging in self-care behaviors, such as exercising and relaxing, as she believed these activities took time away from her work. After reading about the importance of setting boundaries and the negative effects of productivity guilt, Olivia decided to make some changes.

First, Olivia identified the boundaries that needed to be set to improve her productivity and well-being. She realized that her work-life balance was severely skewed and that she needed to make time for her personal life. Olivia began setting specific times to check and respond to emails, ensuring that her workday had a defined start and end time. She also scheduled regular breaks throughout the day, allowing herself to recharge.

To address her perfectionism, Olivia started practicing self-compassion and reframing her negative thoughts about herself. She acknowledged that it was impossible to achieve perfection in every task and that it was more important to focus on progress and growth. This mindset shift helped her feel less guilty when she didn't meet her own high standards.

Olivia also set boundaries with her work, such as not answering calls or messages after 5 pm. This allowed her to prioritize her time and energy for personal activities and self-care. She reconnected with friends, resumed her exercise routine, and spent more time with her family. By doing so, she felt more energized, focused, and motivated during her work hours.

As Olivia continued to set and maintain boundaries, she noticed a significant reduction in stress and guilt. She started to feel more in control of her life and found a healthy work-life balance. With these boundaries in place, she began to achieve her goals without sacrificing her mental and physical well-being.

To overcome productivity guilt, it is essential for us to recognize and reframe negative thoughts and beliefs about ourselves. Setting boundaries is a critical part of increasing productivity and well-being. It involves identifying the boundaries that need to be set to increase productivity and implementing strategies for setting and maintaining boundaries and personal life. Setting boundaries can help us create a healthy work-life balance, prioritize our time and energy, and reduce stress and guilt (Barker, 2016).Setting specific times to check and respond to emails or scheduling regular breaks throughout the day can help us stay focused and productive. Setting boundaries with work, such as not answering calls or messages after a certain time, can also help us prioritize our time and energy (Barker, 2016).

By recognizing and reframing negative thoughts and beliefs, and implementing strategies for setting and maintaining boundaries, we can reduce stress and guilt and increase productivity. By taking care of ourselves and prioritizing our time and energy, we can create a healthy work-life balance and achieve our goals.

The Equilibrium Effect

An imbalanced work-life can be identified by a number of signs, including feeling constantly exhausted, neglecting personal relationships, and feeling stressed or overwhelmed. Common causes of imbalance include long working hours, lack of control over one's schedule, and a lack of support from colleagues or supervisors.

Work-life balance is an important aspect of living a healthy and fulfilling life because it can be difficult to draw the line between work and personal time, especially in today's fast-paced and connected world where it's easy to be connected to work 24/7. However, setting boundaries is crucial for maintaining mental and physical well-being, as well as building strong relationships with family and friends.

The first step in setting boundaries for work-life balance is to identify the areas in which you need to set boundaries. This may include specific times of the day or week when you will not be available for work, activities or hobbies that you want to make time for, and people or activities that are important to you outside of work. Next, it's important to communicate your boundaries to your employer, colleagues, and clients. This may involve setting an "out of office" message on your email, letting your colleagues know when you will not be available, or having a conversation with your manager about your work schedule. Be clear and consistent in your communication, and be prepared to follow through on your boundaries. By planning your day and sticking to it, one hour can be set aside for lunch, breaks, and spending time with your loved ones. This ensures that you are able to take time for yourself and that you are less likely to get caught up in work and neglect other areas of your life. Set boundaries with technology by turning off notifications for work-related apps after hours and limiting your use of social media and other forms of technology. This can help you to disconnect from work and to be present in other areas of your life.

Meet Archer. Archer works long hours at his job and often feels overwhelmed with stress. He's constantly exhausted and finds himself neglecting his personal relationships and hobbies. Archer is struggling to find a healthy work-life balance, and he knows it's taking a toll on his physical and mental health.

Archer realizes that he needs to set boundaries in order to create a better work-life balance for himself. He starts by identifying the areas where he needs to set boundaries, such as specific times of the day when he won't be available for work and activities that he wants to make time for outside of work. Next, Archer communicates his boundaries to his employer and colleagues. He sets an "out of office" message on his email and has a conversation with his manager about his work schedule. Archer is clear and consistent in his communication, and he's prepared to follow through on his boundaries.

By planning his day and sticking to his boundaries, Archer is able to set aside time for lunch, breaks, and spending time with his loved ones. He also sets boundaries with technology by turning off notifications for work-related apps after hours and limiting his use of social media and other forms of technology. Archer knows that setting boundaries is not an easy task, but he's committed to finding the right balance for himself.

Through this process, Archer is able to create a healthier balance between work and personal life, which leads to a more fulfilling and satisfying life overall. He feels better physically and mentally and is able to develop closer bonds with his loved ones. Archer has learned that setting work-life boundaries is critical for maintaining his emotional and physical health, and he's committed to making it a priority in his life.

According to research, a work-life imbalance can have a detrimental effect on one's physical and mental well-being as well as interpersonal relationships. According to one study (Bültmann et al., 2002), long work hours, high job demands, and little job control were linked to higher levels of stress and negative mental health outcomes like anxiety and depression. The study also discovered a link between a poor work-life balance and a higher risk of cardiovascular disease and other chronic illnesses.

It's not an easy task to set boundaries, as it can be challenging to resist the pull of work and to say no to certain tasks or projects. But, remember that setting boundaries is a process, and it may take time to find the right balance for you. It's also important to be flexible and to adjust your boundaries as needed. Setting work-life boundaries is critical for maintaining your emotional and physical health as well as developing close bonds with your loved ones. By identifying areas where boundaries are needed, communicating those boundaries to others, scheduling your time consistently and setting boundaries with technology, you can create a healthier balance between work and personal life, which will ultimately lead to a more fulfilling and satisfying life.

Tips for Maintaining Work-Life Balance

Maintaining a healthy work-life balance can be challenging, especially in a world where technology has made it easier to stay connected to work at all times. However, achieving balance is essential for our well-being, both in our personal and professional lives. Here are 12 tips to help you maintain a healthy work-life balance and lead a fulfilling life.

1. Boundary Setting: To maintain a healthy work-life balance, it's crucial to establish and adhere to set working hours. For instance, if you work from home, establish a schedule that clearly defines your work hours and stick to it.

2. Email Management: Checking and responding to emails can be stressful and disrupt your workflow. Instead, set specific times of the day to check and respond to emails. For example, you could check and respond to emails at specific times during the workday.

3. Scheduled Rest: Taking regular breaks is essential for your well-being. Consider scheduling in breaks throughout your workday, such as taking a 10-minute walk or stretching. For example, you could take a 10-minute break every 90 minutes to recharge and avoid burnout.

4. Goal Orientation: Setting specific goals can help you stay focused and productive. For instance, you could create a to-do list each morning outlining the most important tasks you need to complete that day.

5. Notification Control: Turning off notifications and distractions during your personal time can help you disconnect from work and reduce stress. For example, you could turn off work-related notifications on your phone or computer when you're spending time with family or friends.

6. Mindful Practices: Mindfulness and self-care activities like meditation, yoga, or exercise can help you relax and reduce stress. For example, you could try practicing mindfulness for five minutes each morning before starting your workday.

7. Social Interactions: Spending time with loved ones can help you maintain social connections and promote well-being. For example, you could schedule a weekly game night with your family or plan a weekend getaway with friends.

8. Personal Hobbies: Pursuing hobbies and interests outside of work can help you find joy and fulfillment. For example, you could try learning a new language or instrument in your free time.

9. Routine Establishment: Establishing a daily routine can help you stay organized and reduce stress. For example, you could wake up at the same time each day, exercise, have breakfast, and start your workday at the same time each day.

10. Be Assertive: Learning to say no to non-essential tasks can help you avoid burnout and reduce stress. For example, you could decline to take on additional work projects that don't align with your priorities.

11. Rest Regularly: Taking regular time off can help you recharge and avoid burnout. For example, you could take a week-long vacation every year or plan a long weekend getaway every few months.

12. Work Detachment: Making it a priority to disconnect from work during your personal time can help you find balance and reduce stress. For example, you could practice turning off your phone or computer after work hours to focus on other activities.

A healthy work-life balance is crucial for our overall well-being. By establishing clear boundaries, setting goals, taking breaks, and prioritizing our personal lives, we can achieve balance and lead a more fulfilling life. These 12 tips are just a starting point, but they can be powerful tools for reducing stress, increasing productivity, and enhancing our quality of life. So, take the time to evaluate your work-life balance, set goals, and make adjustments as necessary to ensure you're living a well-balanced life.

Multitasking and Boundary Setting

Multitasking is commonly perceived as a valuable skill, allowing you to handle multiple tasks simultaneously. However, an abundance of research suggests that multitasking can be detrimental to your productivity and overall well-being. When attempting to juggle several tasks, you often lack full concentration on any single task, leading to errors or missed details. Furthermore, task-switching disrupts your brain's ability to focus, resulting in decreased productivity.

To mitigate the negative consequences of multitasking, it is essential for you to establish boundaries and prioritize tasks. By concentrating on one task at a time, you can devote your full attention to each task, ensuring accurate and efficient completion. This focused approach can also alleviate stress, as it eliminates the need for you to constantly balance multiple tasks.

One effective method for setting boundaries around multitasking involves creating a schedule or to-do list. Allocating specific time slots for each task helps you maintain focus and prioritize tasks according to their importance. This strategy ensures that the most crucial tasks are addressed first, promoting a more organized and efficient work approach.

Beyond establishing boundaries for multitasking, it is equally important for you to prioritize self-care and take breaks. Regular breaks help reduce stress and boost productivity by allowing your brain to rest and recharge. This practice can also prevent burnout, a common issue that arises when you engage in constant multitasking without considering your personal well-being.

Consider the case of Simon, an independent real estate agent juggling numerous clients and deadlines. In his attempt to multitask, Simon often answers calls while scheduling property viewings or responds to emails while conducting market research. Despite his efforts, Simon finds himself making mistakes, missing crucial details, and feeling perpetually stressed and overwhelmed. Recognizing that his multitasking habits may be negatively impacting his productivity and well-being, Simon decides to implement boundaries.

Simon begins by crafting a schedule that prioritizes his most important tasks and designates specific times for each. To minimize distractions, he turns off notifications on his devices during work hours and sets clear expectations and boundaries with friends and family. By focusing on one task at a time and limiting interruptions, Simon can fully engage with each task, leading to increased efficiency and accuracy. Additionally, he incorporates breaks throughout the day to rest and recharge, helping him prevent burnout and manage stress levels more effectively.

As a result of these changes, Simon experiences enhanced productivity and efficiency in his work. He feels less stressed and overwhelmed, which in turn allows him to enjoy his free time more fully. Ultimately, by prioritizing tasks and concentrating on one task at a time, Simon achieves an improved work-life balance and overall well-being.

While multitasking may initially appear as a practical approach to work, it often leads to decreased productivity and heightened stress levels. To counteract these negative effects, it is crucial for you to establish boundaries around multitasking. This involves prioritizing tasks, focusing on one task at a time, limiting distractions, and emphasizing self-care. By adopting these strategies, you can enhance your productivity, reduce stress levels, and ultimately achieve a more balanced work-life experience.

Fostering Limits, Nurturing Yourself

Establishing and maintaining healthy boundaries is a crucial aspect of self-care, as it allows us to safeguard our time, energy, and emotional well-being from the demands and expectations of others. By setting clear limits, we enable ourselves to focus on our own needs and priorities, rather than consistently striving to fulfill the desires of those around us.

A primary reason why boundaries are indispensable for self-care is that they help us maintain balance and control in our lives. Without them, we can quickly become overwhelmed by the expectations of others, causing our own needs and desires to be sidelined. This neglect may result in feelings of resentment, burnout, and even physical and emotional exhaustion. However, by implementing boundaries, we can prioritize our well-being and avert these negative consequences.

Clear boundaries not only serve our own well-being, but they also facilitate effective communication of our needs and desires to others, fostering healthy relationships. This can prevent misunderstandings and conflicts, leading to more satisfying and fulfilling connections. To establish these boundaries, various methods can be employed, and the most successful approach will depend on the person and the specific situation. Some effective strategies include learning to say "no" when necessary, setting limits on the time and energy we devote to others, and being clear and direct about our needs and desires. Additionally, it's crucial to practice self-awareness and reflection to recognize toxicity in our relationships.

Creating and maintaining healthy boundaries requires consistency and clear communication. This can be challenging, especially when dealing with people accustomed to having their way, but it is vital for preserving our well-being. By learning to set boundaries, we prioritize our well-being, which is crucial for living a happy and fulfilled life.

Establishing boundaries is also essential for maintaining a healthy work-life balance, reducing stress, and boosting productivity. It empowers you to distinguish between your professional and personal lives, significantly impacting your overall well-being. This separation results in numerous benefits that can positively influence various aspects of your life, such as maintaining a healthy work-life balance. Work can easily consume all your time and energy, leaving little room for personal pursuits and relationships. However, establishing work boundaries allows for a better separation between your professional and personal lives, enabling you to focus on your personal life without being overwhelmed by professional responsibilities. This results in a more fulfilling personal life, positively affecting your mental and physical health.

Constantly thinking about work can lead to burnout and a sense of being overburdened, so creating work-related boundaries reduces stress. Setting clear limits helps you manage your workload and prevent burnout, leading to decreased stress levels and improved overall well-being. These boundaries also enhance productivity, as when you're not always preoccupied with work, you can concentrate on the task at hand, bolstering performance and efficiency.

Furthermore, setting boundaries can foster improved relationships. When you can separate your professional and personal lives, you can better focus on your relationships with family and friends, leading to stronger and more fulfilling connections. This can positively impact overall well-being and prevent conflicts arising from neglecting personal relationships due to work demands.

It is essential to periodically evaluate and adjust your boundaries as your circumstances change. Life transitions, such as starting a new job, entering a new relationship, or having a child, may necessitate re-evaluating your boundaries to maintain a healthy equilibrium. Developing self-awareness and emotional intelligence can also help you recognize when your boundaries need to be redefined. Pay attention to feelings of stress, anxiety, or exhaustion, as they may indicate that your boundaries are being pushed or ignored.

Respecting the boundaries of others is equally important, as it not only contributes to stronger relationships but also creates a culture of mutual respect and understanding. By respecting others' boundaries, you foster an environment where everyone feels valued and heard, which ultimately benefits everyone involved.

Establishing and maintaining healthy boundaries is a vital component of self-care that allows us to preserve our time, energy, and emotional well-being. By setting clear limits, we can achieve balance and control in our lives, cultivate healthy relationships, and prioritize our own needs and desires. By continuously reassessing and adjusting our boundaries, we create a more balanced, fulfilling, and enjoyable life.

Your Happiness Toolkit

Setting and maintaining healthy boundaries is crucial for achieving a healthy work-life balance and managing stress. Here are ten practical tips to help you establish clear boundaries that support your values and priorities, promote productivity, and ensure overall well-being.

1. Reflect on your current boundaries: Take some time to think about the boundaries you currently have in place, such as how much time you spend working, when you are available to answer emails, or how much time you take for self-care. Determine if they are working for you and if they align with your values and priorities.

2. Set goals: Establish specific goals for yourself in regards to your boundaries and work towards achieving them. For example, you could set a goal to take a lunch break every day, to disconnect from work-related technology after a certain time, or to set aside time for self-care each week.

3. Communicate with your employer: Speak with your employer about your boundaries and see if there are any changes that can be made to accommodate them. For example, you could discuss working from home, flexible working hours, or ways to manage your workload.

4. Prioritize self-care: Make sure to prioritize self-care and make time for activities that help you relax and recharge. Examples of self-care activities include exercise, meditation, reading, or spending time with loved ones.

5. Be flexible: Be open to adjusting your boundaries as necessary. Remember that your needs and priorities may change over time, and it's important to be flexible and adapt accordingly. For example, if you find that your workload is increasing and your current boundaries are no longer sustainable, you may need to adjust them.

6. Learn to say 'no': It's important to be able to say no to things that don't align with your boundaries, and to not feel guilty about it. This can include saying no to additional projects, delegating tasks, or declining invitations to social events if they conflict with your boundaries.

7. Keep track of your progress: Keep track of how your boundaries are impacting your work and overall well-being, and make adjustments as needed. For example, you could keep a journal or use a tracking app to monitor your work-life balance, stress levels, or productivity.

8. Learn to set limits: Set limits for yourself in terms of how much work or stress you are willing to take on at any given time. This can include setting a limit on the number of hours you work each day, the number of emails you respond to, or the number of meetings you attend.

9. Define what is important to you: Reflect on what is important to you, whether it be family time, personal growth, or a specific project, and make sure that your boundaries align with your values and priorities. Prioritize what is important to you, and make sure that your boundaries support that.

10. Remember the importance of balance: Maintaining a balance between work and your personal life is crucial for your overall well-being make sure that your boundaries support this balance by allocating enough time for both work and personal activities.

11. Identify and address potential barriers: Reflect on any potential barriers or obstacles that may prevent you from setting or maintaining your boundaries, such as work culture, personal beliefs, or external pressures. Develop strategies to address these barriers and seek support if necessary, to help you overcome these challenges and uphold your boundaries.

12. Educate yourself on the benefits of self-care: Familiarize yourself with the psychological and physical benefits of self-care and establishing healthy boundaries. This knowledge can serve as a powerful motivator to prioritize your well-being and maintain your boundaries consistently.

By reflecting on your current boundaries, setting goals, and communicating with your employer, you can establish healthy boundaries that align with your values and priorities. Prioritizing self-care, being flexible, and learning to say 'no' are also crucial in setting boundaries that work for you. Keep track of your progress, learn to set limits, and define what is important to you. Remember that maintaining a balance between work and personal life is crucial for your overall well-being, and setting boundaries is a key step towards achieving this balance.

Self-Assessment - Assessing Your Current Work-Life Balance

Understanding and maintaining a healthy work-life balance is crucial for our mental and physical well-being. This self-assessment is designed to evaluate your current situation and identify any areas that may need attention. By reflecting on each statement, you will gain a deeper insight into how well you are managing the delicate balance between your professional and personal life.

Please rate your agreement with each statement on a scale of 1 to 5, where 1 = Strongly Disagree, 2 = Disagree, 3 = Neutral, 4 = Agree, and 5 = Strongly Agree.

1. I am able to allocate my time effectively between work and personal life.
2. I feel that my work-related stressors are manageable and do not interfere with my personal life.
3. I often experience guilt when I am not working, even during my personal time.
4. I have clearly defined boundaries between my work and personal life.
5. I feel satisfied with my current work-life balance.

6. I prioritize self-care and personal well-being alongside my work responsibilities.

7. I find it challenging to set and maintain boundaries between work and personal life.

8. Multitasking between work and personal tasks does not negatively impact my overall well-being.

9. I make a conscious effort to nurture my personal relationships and interests outside of work.

10. I am able to "switch off" from work when I am not on the job.

11. I regularly evaluate my time allocation to ensure that my work-life balance is maintained.

12. I have a support system in place to help me manage my work-life balance effectively.

13. I feel comfortable saying "no" to additional work tasks when it would compromise my personal life.

14. I often find myself working during my personal time, even when it is not necessary.

15. I believe that setting boundaries between work and personal life is important for my mental health.

16. I am aware of the signs that indicate my work-life balance may be off and take steps to address them.

17. I feel overwhelmed by my work-related stressors and struggle to find balance in my life.

18. I am proactive in addressing any imbalance between my work and personal life.

19. I make time for activities and hobbies that I enjoy outside of work.

20. I feel confident in my ability to maintain a healthy work-life balance in the long term.

Interpretation

Add up your total score and refer to the following scale:

20-40: Poor Work-Life Balance

Your work-life balance is significantly out of sync. You may be struggling to manage work-related stressors, and your personal life could be suffering as a result. It is important to take steps to address this imbalance and prioritize self-care, personal well-being, and setting boundaries between work and personal life.

41-60: Moderate Work-Life Balance

Your work-life balance is somewhat stable, but there is room for improvement. You may experience occasional challenges managing work-related stressors and maintaining boundaries between work and personal life. Focusing on self-care, setting clear boundaries, and regularly evaluating your time allocation can help enhance your work-life balance.

61-80: Good Work-Life Balance

You have a good work-life balance, with a healthy separation between work and personal life. You manage work-related stressors effectively and prioritize self-care and personal well-being. Continue to maintain your boundaries and nurture your personal interests and relationships to sustain this healthy balance.

81-100: Excellent Work-Life Balance

Your work-life balance is excellent. You have effectively set boundaries between work and personal life, manage work-related stressors, and prioritize self-care and personal well-being. Continue to monitor and adjust your boundaries as needed and maintain your focus on personal interests and relationships to ensure your work-life balance remains optimal.

Self-awareness is the first step towards a healthier work-life balance. The answers you've provided in this self-assessment will help you recognize areas of strength and those that need improvement. Remember, the goal isn't perfection but a sustainable balance that supports your overall well-being and satisfaction in both your personal and professional lives.

Exercise: Assessing Your Current Work-Life Balance

1. What are the signs that your work-life balance is currently off-kilter?
2. Can you identify any work-related stressors that contribute to an unhealthy work-life balance?
3. Reflect on your average week. How much time do you dedicate to work versus personal life? Are you satisfied with this distribution or do you find yourself wishing for more balance?
4. On a scale of 1 to 10, how would you rate your current work-life balance? What key factors contribute to this rating?
5. Can you identify any fears or concerns that might be preventing you from setting boundaries at work? What are the potential risks and benefits of overcoming these fears?
6. What are the driving forces behind your tendency to overwork? Are they internal (e.g., personal ambition, fear of failure) or external (e.g., management pressure, societal expectations)?
7. Have you experienced guilt or anxiety when you are not being productive? How can you challenge these feelings and redefine your understanding of productivity?
8. How often do you find yourself multitasking? How does this impact your work efficiency and stress levels? What boundaries could you set to manage multitasking?
9. What are some personal boundaries you could set to ensure you have time and energy for self-care? How might these boundaries improve your well-being and work performance?
10. What activities or practices bring you joy and relaxation? How can you integrate these into your daily or weekly routine as part of your 'happiness toolkit'?
11. What is one boundary you can set with others to improve your work-life balance? How can you communicate this boundary in a respectful and assertive manner?
12. How do you respond when your work boundaries are tested or violated? What strategies can you use to reinforce these boundaries?

Chapter 5: Thriving in the Digital Age

"You are responsible for your own happiness. You have the power to create boundaries that will protect it." – Jonathan Riley

The Fusion of Technology and Work-Life Balance

We are at the crossroads of technology and work-life balance, where our autonomy and the devices that bind us to our duties perform a complex dance. This fusion, while potent, has the potential to either enhance or encroach on the balance of our lives. It is imperative to remember that you are the choreographer of your own happiness. Harnessing the power to craft boundaries that safeguard your peace is a fundamental attribute of this dance, a performance that can echo into the other areas of your life.

The concept of identifying and respecting your non-negotiables becomes pivotal in this context. These are the sacred aspects of your life, the untouchables that form the foundation of your happiness. Non-negotiables could range from a cherished nightly ritual with your children to a sacred morning run, or perhaps that rare, unbroken hour of solitude with a good book. They are the facets of your life that, if compromised, lead to a sense of dissatisfaction or imbalance. Recognizing and honoring these non-negotiables is a critical step in preserving your work-life balance, especially in an era where technology can effortlessly blur these boundaries.

Periodically, it becomes necessary to review your job description, to realign your work responsibilities with your personal values. Not all tasks carry the same weight or have the same impact. Recognize the activities that truly contribute to your organization's objectives, and those that align with your career goals. This introspection can reveal tasks that are better suited for delegation, freeing up time and mental resources for activities that truly matter to you.

Delegation is not just a managerial tool, but an essential strategy for maintaining balance. It's an acknowledgement that you are part of a collective, and the workload can and should be distributed. Delegation enables you to focus on the tasks that are most meaningful or require your unique expertise, a shift that can lead to increased satisfaction both in and out of work.

As we continue the discourse on work-life balance, we must acknowledge the role of technology as a catalyst for connectivity and efficiency, but also as a potential disruptor of our peace. It presents us with a paradox, a double-edged sword that can either enable or sabotage our efforts to find harmony. It becomes paramount to remember that technology is a tool that we control, not the other way around.

The fusion of technology and work-life balance, while challenging, is manageable. By actively curating our boundaries, respecting our non-negotiables, reviewing and delegating tasks, scheduling breaks, disconnecting from devices, and embracing routines, we can harness technology to serve us, rather than enslave us. It's a dance, and we are the choreographers, empowered to create a masterpiece that resonates with harmony and happiness.

Identify Your Non-Negotiables

Identifying your non-negotiables is a crucial aspect of self-care, especially in today's fast-paced work culture, where burnout and overwhelm are prevalent. It's easy to get caught up in the never-ending to-do lists and the pressure to be always available, but knowing your non-negotiables can help you set healthy boundaries and prevent burnout.

In addition to helping you create boundaries and make better decisions, identifying your non-negotiables can also help you align your actions with your values. When you know what's truly important to you, you can make sure that your actions align with those values. This can bring a sense of purpose and meaning to your work, which can be incredibly motivating.

Another benefit of identifying your non-negotiables is that it can help you make better choices about your career. For example, if you know that spending time with your family is a non-negotiable for you, you can look for jobs that offer more flexibility in terms of working hours or remote work options. Or if you have a non-negotiable around work-life balance, you can prioritize companies that have a culture of respecting their employees' time off and boundaries.

Bianca is a working mom with two young children. One of her non-negotiables is spending quality time with her family. Bianca wants to be present for her children's milestones and wants to create lasting memories with them. She also values her career and wants to succeed in her job. However, she knows that she cannot sacrifice her family time for her career.

So, when Bianca is offered a new job that requires frequent travel and long hours, she takes the time to evaluate whether it aligns with her non-negotiable. She talks to the potential employer about her priorities and whether they can accommodate her family time. After negotiation, the employer agrees to allow her to work from home two days a week and not travel during certain periods, so she can attend her children's important events.

Bianca's non-negotiable of family time helps her prioritize her life and create boundaries. She communicates her boundaries with her employer and makes it clear that her family is her top priority. By doing so, she can make better decisions that align with her values, and she can create a work-life balance that works for her and her family.

Overall, identifying your non-negotiables is about taking ownership of your life and your choices. It's about recognizing what's truly important to you and making sure that you prioritize those things in your life. By doing so, you can create a sense of balance and fulfillment that can positively impact all areas of your life.

Tips to Identify Your Non-Negotiables

Setting boundaries and identifying non-negotiables is crucial to maintaining a healthy balance between the two. By taking the time to reflect on our values, limits, and priorities, we can make informed decisions that align with our personal and professional goals.

1. **Reflect On Your Values:** Take some time to think about what is important to you in your personal and professional life. What values do you hold dear and how do they guide your decision-making?

2. **Set Clear Boundaries:** Once you have identified your non-negotiables, it's important to communicate them to others. This can be as simple as setting clear boundaries around your work schedule or letting others know what types of interactions you are and are not comfortable with.

3. **Consider Your Limits:** Be honest with yourself about what you are and are not comfortable with in terms of workload, interactions with others, and any other potential stressors.

4. **Practice Self-Care:** In order to effectively set and maintain your non- negotiables, it's important to prioritize your own well-being. Make sure to set aside time for self-care and to prioritize your physical and emotional health.

5. **Boundaries:** Setting clear boundaries around what is and is not acceptable in terms of workload, communication, and expectations is a key way to identify your non-negotiables. For example, you may not be willing to work overtime or on weekends, or you may not be willing to work with certain types of clients.

6. **Values:** Identifying your core values and what you stand for is another way to identify your non-negotiables. For example, if you value honesty and integrity, you may not be willing to work for a company that has a history of unethical practices.

7. **Priorities:** Understanding what is most important to you in terms of your career goals and aspirations can help you identify your non-negotiables. For example, if career advancement is a priority, you may not be willing to work for a company that does not have clear opportunities for growth.

8. **Work-life balance:** Ensuring that your work does not consume your entire life is important to many people, and can be a non-negotiable. For example, you may not be willing to take on a job that requires you to travel frequently or have a flexible schedule.

9. **Compensation:** Money is often a big consideration when it comes

to work, and your compensation package can be a non-negotiable. For example, you may not be willing to work for less than a certain salary or benefits package.

10. **Professional development:** Investing in your own professional development is important for many people, and can be a non-negotiable. For example, you may not be willing to work for a company that does not provide opportunities for training or education.

11. **Company culture:** The culture and values of a company can play a big role in how satisfied you are in your job, and may be a non-negotiable for you. For example, you may not be willing to work for a company that does not have a positive and inclusive work environment.

12. **Team dynamics:** The dynamics of the team you work with can greatly impact your job satisfaction and may be a non-negotiable. For example, you may not be willing to work with a team that is not cohesive or lacks strong leadership.

By understanding what is important to us and what we are and are not willing to compromise on, we can make choices that align with our values and goals. Remember to practice self-care, communicate your boundaries to others, and prioritize your well-being as you navigate your personal and professional life.

The Art of Prioritizing

Life is a complex and ever-changing journey, filled with competing demands and responsibilities. In the midst of these, work often assumes a predominant role, which can blur the boundaries between professional and personal life. To lead a fulfilling and harmonious life, it is essential to identify and prioritize the aspects that hold true importance for you. Establishing boundaries allows you to focus on your core values, aligning your actions to achieve lasting happiness and success, and ensuring that work doesn't overshadow other important facets of life.

Taking care of your physical and mental health should be a top priority, as it allows you to enjoy life and be productive at work. It is the backbone that supports your productivity, both personal and professional, and ability to savor life's offerings. To establish boundaries for holistic health, set aside time for regular exercise, a balanced diet, and sufficient rest. By doing so, you will be better prepared to handle a rigors work schedule.

Equally important to your overall satisfaction and well-being are the relationships you nurture with family and friends. As work becomes a priority for most people, these emotional bonds can sometimes take a backseat. To counteract this, allocate time to connect with your loved ones, and establish boundaries that separate work from your personal life. In cultivating these meaningful connections, you infuse your life with richness and create a supportive network that can help you navigate professional challenges.

Work is often seen as a means to financial stability, a crucial aspect of life. While it's essential for meeting basic needs, it also requires thoughtful management and future planning. To prioritize this, devise a budget, accumulate savings, eliminate debt, and invest in your financial future. Set boundaries that encourage sound financial habits, like ensuring work doesn't push these important considerations to the side.

Emotional boundaries form a critical component of self-care and personal growth, particularly as work stressors can often affect emotional health. To prioritize emotional well-being, stay attuned to your feelings and needs, both at work and at home, and assertively communicate them to others. Empower yourself to say "no" when required at work, ensuring you don't stretch yourself thin to satisfy professional demands at the expense of personal life.

Work often becomes a priority for most people, but understanding and prioritizing the diverse dimensions of your life is instrumental for a harmonious and fulfilling life. By consciously directing attention towards health, relationships, personal growth, and other significant areas, you can sculpt a life that personifies your values and goals. Establishing boundaries and prioritizing your time empowers you to nurture all life aspects, fostering a sense of balance and contentment, and ensuring that work serves your life, not the other way around. Remember, the pursuit of a balanced life is a dynamic process; regularly reassess your priorities and make the necessary adjustments to manifest the life you envisage.

While work often becomes a priority, it's also important to nurture other aspects that contribute to a rounded life experience, such as indulging in activities that spark joy. These activities offer a deep sense of fulfillment and serve as a sanctuary to unwind from daily pressures, including those stemming from work. To give your hobbies and personal interests the time they deserve, ensure they find a place in your routine. Set boundaries that safeguard this time, allowing you to immerse in your passions without work-related interruptions. By allocating time to pursuits you love, you cultivate a reservoir of joy and satisfaction, contributing to a harmonious and fulfilling life.

A sense of purpose and fulfillment often emerges from contributing to the community and aiding others. In the hustle of meeting work deadlines and targets, it's easy to sideline these altruistic commitments. To prioritize philanthropy, identify the causes close to your heart and discover ways to offer your support. Establish boundaries that allow you to balance altruistic commitments with work and personal needs, ensuring your acts of kindness are sustainable and impactful. By investing in generosity, you enrich your own life while making a positive difference in the world around you.

It is important to acknowledge the fluid nature of life and the subsequent evolution of your priorities over time. Work priorities may fluctuate, and personal interests can shift. To maintain equilibrium, frequently reassess your priorities and make necessary adjustments to adapt to changing circumstances or ambitions. Embrace a mindset of flexibility and adaptability, allowing yourself to grow and evolve in tandem with your life journey. By being receptive to change and adjusting your boundaries as required, you can persistently craft a life reflective of your values and aspirations, with work being a part, but not all, of your life.

Ultimately, while work is a significant part of life, it should not overshadow or disrupt other equally important aspects. By setting clear boundaries, you can ensure that work enriches your life, rather than detracts from it. This approach leads to a more balanced, fulfilling life, where work is one of many priorities, each receiving the attention and time it deserves. Through this, you can achieve a harmonious blend of professional success and personal contentment.

Crafting the Perfect Balance

It is crucial to identify and prioritize the aspects of life that hold true importance for you. By focusing on your core values and aligning your actions, you can achieve lasting happiness and success. The following points provide strategies to help you prioritize key areas of your life, such as personal well-being, relationships, growth, and financial stability.

1. **Health & Well-Being:** Taking care of your physical and mental health should be a top priority, as it allows you to enjoy life and be productive. This can include regular exercise, a balanced diet, and getting enough sleep.

2. **Personal Relationships:** Maintaining strong relationships with family and friends is important for your overall happiness and well-being. Make time to spend with the people you care about whether it's through regular catch-ups or special occasions.

3. **Hobbies & Personal Interests:** Engaging in activities you enjoy can provide a sense of fulfillment and help you relax and unwind after a long day. Whether it's reading, painting, or playing a musical instrument, make sure to set aside time for your hobbies.

4. **Personal Growth & Development:** Continuously learning and improving can help you stay motivated and engaged. This can include taking courses, learning new skills, or pursuing personal projects.

5. **Giving Back:** Many people find a sense of purpose and fulfillment by contributing to their community or helping others. This can be through volunteering, donating to charities, or supporting causes you care about.

6. Financial Stability: While earning an income is necessary for meeting your basic needs, it's also important to manage your money wisely and plan for the future. This can include setting aside savings, paying off debt, and investing in your financial security.

7. Making the Most of Your Days: Effective time management is essential to achieving balance in your life. To prioritize your time, create a daily or weekly schedule that allocates time for work, personal relationships, hobbies, personal growth, and self-care.

8. Achieving Harmony between Career and Personal Life: By striking a balance between career and personal life, you can enjoy the rewards of a successful career while nurturing your overall well-being. Set clear boundaries between your professional and personal life, such as having specific work hours, avoiding work-related tasks during personal time, and communicating your needs to colleagues and family members.

9. Protecting Your Inner Peace: By cultivating emotional boundaries, you empower yourself to maintain inner peace and foster healthy relationships. Establishing emotional boundaries is an essential aspect of self-care and personal growth. To prioritize emotional well-being, be aware of your feelings and needs, and communicate them assertively to others.

10. Embracing Change and Growth: By being open to change and adjusting your boundaries as needed, you can continue to create a life that embodies your values and goals. Recognize that life is ever-changing and that your priorities may shift over time. To maintain balance, regularly re-evaluate your priorities and make necessary adjustments to accommodate changes in your circumstances or goals.

Recognizing and prioritizing various facets of your life is vital for a harmonious and fulfilling existence. By consciously directing attention towards health, relationships, personal growth, and other important areas, you can create a life that embodies your values and goals. Remember, pursuing a balanced life is an ongoing process; regularly re-evaluate your priorities and make necessary adjustments to live the life you envision.

Review Your Job Description

In today's rapidly evolving and demanding work environment, maintaining a healthy work-life balance is more important than ever. To achieve this balance, setting boundaries and clearly defining job responsibilities are crucial steps. By being cognizant of your limitations and effectively communicating them, you can ensure optimal performance at work while preserving your well-being.

Establishing boundaries is essential for creating a cohesive and efficient workplace where everyone understands their roles and responsibilities. One way to achieve this objective is by regularly reviewing your job description. As your role evolves over time, it's important to update your job description to ensure it accurately reflects your current responsibilities. This clarity helps prevent confusion, misunderstandings, and potential conflicts within the team.

Research supports the benefits of setting boundaries, indicating that it can improve job satisfaction and reduce the risk of burnout (Grawitch, M.J., Werth, P.M., Palmer, S.N., 2018). If you find yourself taking on additional work beyond your job description, it's vital to discuss the situation with your employer. This conversation can help determine whether the extra work is necessary and should be incorporated into your job description or if it falls outside your purview and should be delegated to someone else.

In some cases, co-workers may be unaware of the extra work you're doing; in others, they might be deliberately avoiding certain tasks. Regardless of the reason, addressing the issue openly and honestly with your supervisor is the most effective way to ensure fair distribution of responsibilities. This approach not only fosters a positive work environment but also guarantees that tasks are completed in a timely and efficient manner.

Setting boundaries also involves protecting your personal time and space outside of work. Research has shown that employees who successfully maintain a healthy work-life balance are more productive and satisfied in their jobs (Greenhaus, J.H., Powell, G.N., 2006). This balance can be achieved by setting specific times for work and personal activities, learning to say "no" to nonessential tasks, and engaging in regular self-care.

Another essential aspect of reviewing your job description is understanding your rights as an employee. Familiarize yourself with your company's policies and any applicable labor laws to ensure you're being treated fairly and are not being exploited. This knowledge will empower you to advocate for yourself and maintain a healthy work-life balance.

Consider the case of Tamara, a dedicated marketing professional who had been working for a mid-sized tech company for three years. As the company grew, so did her workload. Initially hired as a Social Media Specialist, her responsibilities began to expand over time. She found herself not only managing the company's social media presence but also creating content for blogs, coordinating email campaigns, and even working on the design aspects of marketing materials.

Tamara's job description, however, had not been updated since she was hired. As a result, she was often overwhelmed by her workload, struggling to balance her professional and personal life. Her stress levels began to rise, and she noticed a decline in her overall well-being.

Realizing that she needed to set boundaries, Tamara took the initiative to review her job description and make a list of all the tasks she was currently responsible for. She also researched the typical responsibilities of a Social Media Specialist and compared them to her actual duties. The discrepancy was striking.

Armed with this information, Tamara scheduled a meeting with her supervisor to discuss her concerns. She presented her findings, explaining that her current workload was beyond the scope of her initial job description, and that the added responsibilities were affecting her work-life balance.

Tamara's supervisor acknowledged the issue and appreciated her proactive approach. Together, they updated her job description, redistributing some tasks to other team members and ensuring that her workload was more manageable. With clear boundaries established and her job description accurately reflecting her responsibilities, Tamara was able to regain control over her work-life balance, perform more effectively in her role, and contribute to a more harmonious workplace.

Setting boundaries is critical for personal well-being and professional success. By regularly reviewing and updating your job description, effectively communicating with your employer and co-workers, and understanding your rights as an employee, you can create a supportive work environment where everyone's responsibilities are clearly defined. This clarity not only helps prevent stress and burnout but also contributes to a more efficient, productive, and harmonious workplace.

Tips for Reviewing Your Job Description

It is critical to review your job description in order to maintain a healthy work-life balance, manage workload, and avoid burnout. Understanding your job responsibilities and identifying areas where boundaries can be set can help you prioritise your work and focus on achieving your objectives. Here are ten practical methods for establishing boundaries.

1. Highlight key responsibilities: Identify the main responsibilities outlined in your job description and make a list of them. This will help you understand what is expected of you and set boundaries based on those expectations.

2. Identify areas of overlap: Look for areas where your job responsibilities may overlap with other team members or departments. This will help you understand where you need to set boundaries to ensure that you are not taking on more than you can handle.

3. Identify areas of flexibility: Look for areas where your job description allows for flexibility or where you can use your own discretion. This will help you understand where you can set boundaries and make decisions based on your own needs and priorities.

4. Identify areas of growth: Look for areas where your job description allows for growth and development. This will help you understand where you can set boundaries and focus on developing your skills and expertise.

5. Communicate with your employer: Have a conversation with your employer to discuss your job description and set boundaries. This will help ensure that you are on the same page and that your supervisor understands your needs and priorities.

6. Identify time constraints: Review your job description to understand the expected time commitments and deadlines. This will help you set boundaries around your work schedule and ensure that you are not overworking yourself.

7. Identify specific tasks and projects: Review your job description to understand the specific tasks and projects that you will be working on. This will help you set boundaries around your workload and ensure that you are not taking on more than you can handle.

8. Understand company policies: Review your job description and company policies to understand the expectations around work-life balance, overtime, and remote work. This will help you set boundaries around your work schedule and ensure that you are adhering to company policies.

9. Identify areas of stress: Look for areas in your job description that may cause stress or burnout. This will help you set boundaries around your workload and take steps to manage stress and maintain your well-being.

10. Seek feedback: Regularly seek feedback from your colleagues to understand how you are meeting the expectations outlined in your job description. This will help you set boundaries and make adjustments as needed to ensure that you are meeting expectations and achieving your goals.

Setting boundaries is essential for achieving success and maintaining your well-being. By understanding your job responsibilities, identifying areas of overlap, flexibility, growth, time constraints, and stress, and communicating with your employer, you can set boundaries that work for you and help you achieve your goals.

Achieving More through Delegation

Delegation serves as a vital component in establishing boundaries, as it enables the distribution of responsibilities, ultimately alleviating your workload. When inundated with an overwhelming number of tasks and projects, the urge to tackle everything singlehandedly can be strong. However, attempting to do so is not only unfeasible, but it also falls short of being an effective leadership approach. Delegating tasks to others permits you to allocate your time and energy to the responsibilities that only you can fulfill while simultaneously offering your team members the chance to enhance their skills and assume greater responsibility.

To delegate proficiently, it is essential to relinquish the notion that you must personally accomplish everything. This can prove challenging, particularly for those accustomed to maintaining control and micromanaging all aspects of their work. Nevertheless, trust constitutes a fundamental element of delegation. Believing in your team members' ability to competently execute their duties and tackle the tasks you assign to them is crucial.

Upon mastering the art of letting go and trusting your team, you can begin to delegate tasks more effectively. Start by pinpointing the most critical responsibilities that require your undivided attention, and proceed to assign the remaining tasks to your team members. Ensure you cater to their individual strengths and capabilities by assigning tasks they can confidently complete. This approach not only guarantees the work is executed to a high standard but also fosters a motivated and contented team environment.

Mastering the skill of effective delegation is essential, as it allows you to concentrate on tasks exclusive to your expertise while simultaneously fostering the development and growth of your team members. By embracing the art of letting go and having confidence in the abilities of others, you can successfully delegate tasks and accomplish greater feats as a cohesive unit.

Delegation offers numerous benefits, including improved time management, team development, and equitable workload distribution.

Consider the example of Shinai, a project manager for a software development company. As the team leader, she is responsible for overseeing the entire project lifecycle, from initial planning to final deployment. Initially, Shinai attempted to manage every aspect of the project herself, including design, development, testing, and client communication. She quickly became overwhelmed and realized that her approach was not sustainable.

Recognizing the importance of delegation, Shinai decided to change her strategy. She began by identifying the most critical tasks that required her personal attention, such as defining the project scope, establishing deadlines, and managing client expectations. She then evaluated the strengths and expertise of her team members and assigned the remaining tasks accordingly.

For instance, Shinai delegated design tasks to her creative team members who excelled in graphic design and user experience. She entrusted the software development to her skilled programmers and assigned the testing responsibilities to team members with keen attention to detail and quality assurance expertise. She also involved her more communicative team members in client communication and progress reporting.

By delegating tasks based on her team members' strengths and capabilities, Shinai not only alleviated her workload but also fostered an environment where her team could grow and develop their skills. Her team members felt empowered and motivated, as they were trusted with important responsibilities and given the opportunity to demonstrate their abilities. This led to increased job satisfaction, improved collaboration, and a more efficient project execution.

A study conducted by Müller and Turner (2005) found that effective delegation plays a critical role in project success. Their research demonstrated that project managers who effectively delegated tasks to their team members had higher project success rates compared to those who did not delegate or delegated ineffectively.

Delegation is a powerful leadership tool that, when executed correctly, offers numerous benefits to both the leader and the team. By learning to trust in the capabilities of others and letting go of the desire to control every aspect of work, you can create a more efficient, motivated, and successful team. Embrace delegation as a means to unlock your team's full potential and pave the way for collective growth and accomplishment.

Tips for Effective Delegation

Delegation is an essential skill for effective leadership and team management. By entrusting tasks to team members, leaders can focus on higher-level responsibilities while empowering their team to develop skills, build confidence, and contribute to the overall success of the project. Here are 12 key steps for successful delegation.

1. Clearly define the task: Clearly communicate the task, its objectives and the expected outcome to the team member who will be responsible for completing it. This includes providing detailed instructions, any specific requirements or standards that need to be met, and any relevant deadlines.

2. Assign ownership: Assign ownership of the task to a specific team member and make sure they understand the importance and the impact of the task on the overall project. This includes giving them the authority and autonomy to make decisions related to the task, and holding them accountable for the final outcome.

3. Establish deadlines: Establish clear deadlines for completing the task and provide regular updates on progress. This includes setting intermediate deadlines for specific milestones, and regularly reviewing progress to ensure that the task is on track.

4. Provide necessary resources: Ensure that the team member has all the necessary resources, such as tools, equipment, and information, to complete the task. This includes providing any necessary software, access to databases or other information sources.

5. Provide support and guidance: Provide support and guidance throughout the task, and be available to answer any questions or address any concerns. This includes providing feedback on progress, offering suggestions for improvement, and addressing any roadblocks that may arise.

6. Monitor progress: Monitor progress regularly and provide feedback on areas that need improvement. This includes setting up regular check-ins or status updates, and providing constructive criticism and guidance on areas where the team member may need to improve.

7. Hold team members accountable: Hold team members accountable for completing the task on time and to the best of their abilities. This includes setting expectations for quality, timeliness, and level of detail, and holding team members responsible for meeting these expectations.

8. Provide recognition: Recognize and reward team members for their efforts and contributions. This includes providing positive feedback, acknowledging their contributions, and offering incentives or bonuses for meeting or exceeding expectations.

9. Establish clear communication: Establish clear communication channels, such as regular meetings, email, or instant messaging, to keep team members informed and to facilitate collaboration. This includes setting up regular check-ins or status updates, and providing clear and timely communication on any changes or updates to the task.

10. Encourage autonomy: Encourage team members to take ownership of the task and to use their own initiative to complete it. This includes giving them the autonomy to make decisions related to the task, and allowing them to use their own methods and techniques to complete it.

11. Delegate to the right person: Delegate tasks to the team member who is best suited to complete them, taking into account their skills, experience, and workload. This includes evaluating each team member's strengths and weaknesses, and assigning tasks that align with their skills and experience.

12. Set clear expectations: Set clear expectations for the quality, timeliness, and level of detail required for the task, and make sure team members understand them. This includes providing detailed instructions, any specific requirements or standards that need to be met, and any relevant deadlines.

Effective delegation is crucial for the success of any project and the growth of team members. By following the 12 steps leaders can ensure tasks are delegated to the right person, clear expectations are set, and team members are supported throughout the process. This not only leads to better project outcomes but also fosters a sense of autonomy and ownership among team members, ultimately strengthening the overall team dynamic and productivity.

The Wisdom in Taking Time to Respond

We, who struggle with setting proper boundaries, often have difficulty asserting ourselves and protecting our time and well-being. This could be due to our desire to please others or to avoid conflict. We might feel guilty, anxious, or uncomfortable when faced with requests and may be quick to agree just to alleviate these feelings. Our tendency to prioritize the needs and expectations of others over our own often leads to a pattern of overcommitment, which then results in increased stress and diminished focus on our own goals and priorities.

Not responding immediately to requests is often attributed to the fear of being seen as uncooperative or unhelpful. This fear can lead us to hastily agree to requests without properly assessing our capacity to fulfill the commitment. The pressure to be seen as a team player, along with concerns about possible repercussions for refusing, makes it challenging for us to assert our own needs and limits. However, by understanding the root of this behavior and recognizing the importance of setting healthy boundaries, we can begin to break the cycle of overcommitment and develop a more balanced approach to managing our time and energy.

A key element of achieving this balance is setting boundaries and being mindful of our time and commitments. By taking the time to thoughtfully respond to requests, we can avoid overcommitting and safeguard our well-being, leading to improved performance and reduced stress. When requests come our way, a considered response allows us to evaluate our current workload, commitments, and priorities. This deliberate approach helps us not only avoid overcommitting but also ensures that we can deliver better-quality work for the tasks we choose to accept. Taking time to respond also fosters a more professional image, showcasing our ability to manage our time effectively and be reliable. This also leads to making more informed decisions regarding our commitments, ensuring efficient allocation of our resources.

Faced with a new request or opportunity, it's important to resist the urge to respond immediately. Instead, we should pause to consider our current obligations and priorities. This thoughtful approach prevents hasty decisions and allows us to review our schedule, workload, and upcoming deadlines to determine if we have the capacity to take on additional tasks. We should consider the time and effort required for the new commitment and how it might affect our existing responsibilities.

We should reflect on how accepting the new commitment might impact our work-life balance and whether it aligns with our personal and professional goals. Weighing the potential benefits and drawbacks before making a decision is essential. Once we've evaluated the request, we should provide a clear, honest response. If we can't commit, we should politely decline and, if possible, offer an alternative solution or recommend someone else who might be able to help. By being transparent and sincere, we demonstrate professionalism and respect for both our own boundaries and the needs of the person making the request.

Let's take the example of Charlotte, a dedicated marketing manager, often found herself feeling overwhelmed by her workload. She had a habit of immediately agreeing to any request that came her way, whether it was from her manager, colleagues, or clients. This led to a significant amount of stress and a negative impact on her work-life balance. However, Charlotte decided to try implementing the "Take Time to Respond" approach in her professional life to regain control over her commitments.

One day, Charlotte received an urgent request to create a new marketing campaign within a short timeframe. Instead of impulsively saying yes, she took a step back and evaluated her current obligations, deadlines, and the effort required to complete the new project. By doing so, Charlotte realized that taking on this additional task would jeopardize the quality of her existing projects and strain her work-life balance even further.

Considering the potential consequences, Charlotte decided to have an open and honest conversation with her supervisor. She explained her current workload and the potential risks of overcommitting. Instead of outright declining the request, she proposed an alternative solution that involved redistributing some of her tasks to colleagues with more availability, ensuring the marketing campaign would still be completed on time.

This experience taught Charlotte the value of taking the time to respond thoughtfully to requests. By doing so, she was able to maintain her boundaries, prioritize her well-being, and focus on delivering quality work. This approach not only improved her work-life balance but also enhanced her professional reputation and her ability to manage her time effectively. In turn, Charlotte felt more empowered and confident in her decision-making, ultimately leading to a healthier and more fulfilling professional life.

By practicing these steps, we will be able to maintain our boundaries, prioritize our well-being, and ensure that we can focus on what truly matters. Taking time to respond allows us to make informed decisions that contribute to a healthier, more balanced lifestyle. Embracing this approach will not only improve our work-life balance but also enhance our overall productivity and professional reputation.

Patience and Poise

Effective communication is crucial in personal and professional settings, and it requires thoughtful responses. However, in the heat of the moment, it can be challenging to think clearly and respond appropriately. Therefore, it is important to have techniques that help you gather your thoughts and respond effectively. Here are 12 techniques that can help you improve your communication skills.

1. The technique of pausing: This involves taking a moment to collect your thoughts before responding to someone. For example, if a colleague asks you a question that you need time to think about, you can say "Let me think about that for a moment" before responding.

2. Take a deep breath: Taking a deep breath can help you to relax and calm your mind before responding. This can help you to think more clearly and respond in a more measured way.

3. Write down your thoughts: If you need more time to organize your thoughts, you can write them down on a piece of paper before responding. This can help you to think more clearly and respond in a more organized way.

4. Ask clarifying questions: If you're not sure what someone is asking or what they're trying to say, you can ask them to clarify their question or statement before responding. This can help you to better understand what they're saying and respond more effectively.

5. Take a walk: Sometimes, stepping away from a situation for a few minutes can help you to clear your head and come up with a better response.

6. Reflect on your emotions: Be mindful of your emotions and how it may be affecting your response. Reflect on the reason why you may be feeling the way you are before responding.

7. Repeat the question or statement: Before responding, repeat the question or statement that was made to ensure that you understand it correctly. This also gives you a moment to gather your thoughts and come up with a response.

8. Use reflective listening: Reflective listening is a technique in which you repeat back to the speaker what they've said, in your own words. This can help to clarify their message, and also give you time to think about your response.

9. Practice active listening: Focus on truly hearing and understanding what your co-worker is saying before formulating a response. By being present and engaged in the conversation, you're more likely to respond thoughtfully and effectively.

10. Prioritize your thoughts: When you have multiple points to make, organize them in your mind before responding. Determine which points are most important and address them first to ensure a clear and concise response.

11. Visualize your response: Before speaking, try to visualize what you want to say and how you want to say it. This mental rehearsal can help you articulate your thoughts more effectively and with greater confidence.

12. Seek feedback: After responding, ask your co-worker for their thoughts or feedback on your response. This can help you gauge whether your communication was effective and can help you improve your communication skills in the future.

Remember, taking time before responding can help you to communicate more effectively and reduce misunderstandings. It also shows that you are thoughtful and considerate in your communication style.

The Art of Stepping Back

Setting aside time away from work is an indispensable aspect of establishing boundaries and safeguarding your mental, emotional, and physical well-being. However, orchestrating a successful break from work can be a daunting task, particularly when juggling a hectic schedule filled with competing priorities. It is vital to recognize that time off is a well-deserved reward, akin to the income you earn through your hard work and dedication. As such, you should never feel guilty about stepping away from your obligations – you've genuinely earned the right to relax and recharge.

To ensure that you actually benefit from your time off and reap the full rewards of your break, consider meticulously planning your vacation or mental health days well in advance. By doing so, you not only create an event to eagerly anticipate but also guarantee that the necessary time is reserved in your calendar, making it less likely that you'll be tempted to postpone or cancel your plans. In addition, having a clear and detailed plan helps to alleviate stress and allows you to fully disconnect from work-related matters during your break, granting you the mental space to truly relax.

When planning your time off, consider selecting a destination or activity that genuinely excites you or offers a chance for personal growth. Whether it's exploring a new city, immersing yourself in nature, or taking up a new hobby, engaging in activities that bring you joy and offer opportunities for self-discovery can make your time off even more meaningful and restorative.

When your time off finally arrives, make a conscious effort to focus on relaxation and rejuvenation. Indulge in self-care practices, such as meditation, yoga, or exercise, to help restore your mind and body. Spend quality time with loved ones to strengthen personal connections, or simply allow yourself the luxury of a guilt-free empower you to return to work feeling revitalized, inspired, and prepared to face any challenges that lie ahead.

Taking time off is an indispensable component of sustaining a healthy work-life balance. It is crucial to recognize that taking breaks does not signify weakness or a lack of dedication; rather, it demonstrates self-awareness and a commitment to long-term personal and professional success. By prioritizing your well-being, you will be better equipped to handle stress and maintain a positive outlook, which in turn can improve your relationships with colleagues and enhance overall workplace satisfaction.

Moreover, setting an example by prioritizing your mental and physical health may inspire others around you to do the same, fostering a healthier and more supportive work environment. Encouraging a culture of self-care and balance can lead to increased productivity, improved morale, and reduced burnout among your peers.

By proactively planning and optimizing your time off, you can effectively safeguard your well-being and ensure that you bring your best self to work upon your return. In the long run, this practice will not only enhance your personal life but also contribute to greater productivity, creativity, and success in your professional endeavors.

For instance, imagine you have always been passionate about photography but never found the time to fully delve into it. You decide to use your upcoming vacation to attend a week-long photography workshop in a picturesque location, allowing you to explore your interests, develop new skills, and create lasting memories.

During your time off, you immerse yourself in the world of photography, connect with like-minded individuals, and enjoy the stunning landscapes that surround you. This experience not only allows you to temporarily disconnect from your work obligations but also fosters personal growth, reigniting your creative spirit and passion for life.

A study from the Harvard Business Review reported that employees who took more vacation time were more likely to receive promotions and raises, suggesting that well-rested individuals are more productive and efficient in their work. These findings emphasize the value of taking time off not only for personal well-being but also for professional growth and success.

Taking time off and prioritizing your well-being is an essential aspect of maintaining a healthy work-life balance. By planning your vacations or mental health days with care and intention, you can create a more meaningful and rejuvenating experience that will leave you feeling refreshed and reinvigorated. Remember to be mindful of your needs and listen to your body – it will often signal when it's time for a break. Embrace the opportunity to disconnect from work, explore new experiences, and cultivate a deeper sense of self-awareness and personal growth.

Tips for Planning Time Off

Orchestrating and managing your time off can be an intricate undertaking, especially when striving to ensure a seamless transition both before and after your absence. Here are ten insightful tips designed to empower you to skillfully navigate your time off, allowing you to fully decompress and rejuvenate with the assurance that all is taken care of.

1. Set aside a specific amount of time: Decide how much time you want to take off and block it out on your calendar. This will help you to commit to taking the time off and ensure that you don't accidentally overbook yourself.

2. Plan activities or relaxation time: Once you have your time off planned, consider what you would like to do during that time. This could include taking a vacation, going on a trip, or simply taking some time for yourself to relax and recharge.

3. Choose a time that works best for you: Consider your work schedule, any upcoming deadlines, and any other commitments you may have when choosing a time to take off. Choose a time when you will be able to fully relax and enjoy your time away from work.

4. Create a plan: Before taking time off, it's important to create a plan that outlines what you need to do before you leave, what will happen while you're away, and what needs to be done upon your return. This should include a list of tasks to be completed, deadlines, and who will be responsible for completing them.

5. Communicate with your team: Let your team members know when you will be away and how to contact you in case of an emergency. This can be done through an email, team meeting or a personal chat. Assign tasks or responsibilities to other team members to ensure that everything runs smoothly while you're away. It's also important to let them know your expectations and what they should do if any urgent situation arise.

6. Tie up loose ends: Before leaving, take care of any unfinished projects or tasks to avoid coming back to a pile of work. This could include submitting reports, finalizing projects, or wrapping up any ongoing initiatives.

7. Set boundaries: Make sure to set boundaries with your team and let them know that you will not be available during your time off. This will help them to not expect a response from you and also it will help you to not feel guilty or stressed about not responding.

8. Disconnect: Make sure to disconnect from work while you are away, so you can truly relax and recharge during your time off. This could mean turning off your work phone or email notifications, or avoiding checking in on work-related tasks or conversations while on vacation.

9. Prepare your work environment: Make sure your work area is clean and organized before you leave, so it's easier for you to pick up where you left off when you return. This could include filing paperwork, cleaning off your desk, and organizing your computer files.

10. Prepare for your return: Before you leave, plan out what you'll need to do when you return, such as catching up on emails, meeting with your team, or resuming regular responsibilities. This could include scheduling meetings, reviewing any updates or changes that occurred during your absence, and setting priorities for your return.

11. Reflect on your time off: After returning from your break, take some time to reflect on your experience. Consider what you enjoyed most, what you learned, and what you would like to incorporate into your daily life moving forward. This will help you make the most of your time off and maintain a healthy work-life balance.

12. Ease back into work: Instead of jumping straight back into your usual routine, give yourself a bit of time to ease back into work. This could mean starting with smaller tasks or setting aside time to catch up with colleagues and updates. This gradual approach can help you better manage the transition and reduce the potential for burnout.

Taking time off is essential for your overall well-being and productivity at work. By following these ten tips, you can prepare yourself, your team, and your work environment for your time away, ensuring that you make the most of your break. Remember to set boundaries and disconnect from work during your time off, so you can truly rejuvenate and return to work with renewed energy and focus. With proper planning and communication, you can enjoy a stress-free vacation and a seamless transition back into your daily routine.

The Essentiality of Taking Breaks

If you ever feel guilty or anxious about taking breaks from work, you're not alone. Many people struggle with these feelings, but it's important to push past them and not skip your breaks. Breaks are crucial for giving your mind and body a chance to recover from work-related stress. This recovery process can help boost your performance and energy levels, which can ultimately help you be more productive. We experience guilt or anxiety when it comes to taking breaks from work, but it's crucial for us to overcome these feelings and prioritize regular rest periods. Breaks serve an essential role in allowing our minds and bodies to recover from work-related stress. In fact, studies have shown that taking short, frequent breaks can enhance productivity and overall well-being, benefiting both employees and organizations alike.

One notable study conducted by the Draugiem Group found that people who took regular breaks throughout the day were more productive than those who worked for longer stretches without interruption. They discovered that the optimal work-to-break ratio was 52 minutes of work followed by a 17-minute break. This approach allows for periods of intense focus, followed by time for mental and physical recuperation.

Taking breaks is not an indication of weakness or laziness. On the contrary, it demonstrates self-awareness, discipline, and a commitment to personal well-being. Embracing regular breaks is a key aspect of maintaining a healthy work-life balance and sustaining long-term productivity.

One of the reasons we might avoid taking breaks is the pervasive "hustle culture" that glorifies overwork and promotes the idea that success requires constant exertion. However, the negative consequences of burnout, including reduced efficiency, lower job satisfaction, and increased health risks, ultimately undermine this narrative.

It's important for us to recognize the value of breaks and to incorporate them into our daily routines. If we find ourselves frequently forgetting to take breaks, we should consider setting reminders in our digital calendars or using a time management app that incorporates break periods. These tools can help ensure that we're giving ourselves the time and space necessary to recharge.

For example, the Pomodoro Technique, a popular time management method, advocates for breaking work into 25-minute intervals, called "pomodoros," followed by a 5-minute break. After completing four pomodoros, a longer break of 15-30 minutes is recommended. This system not only helps maintain focus during work periods but also encourages regular rest, fostering a more balanced and sustainable approach to productivity.

Wyatt, a dedicated software developer, had always been a firm believer in the "hustle culture." He would often work long hours without taking breaks, thinking that this approach would make him more productive and successful. As time went on, however, Wyatt began to feel the effects of burnout, including increased stress, a lack of focus, and a decline in his overall well-being.

Realizing that his approach to work was unsustainable, Wyatt decided to implement regular breaks into his routine. He adopted the Pomodoro Technique, dividing his work into 25-minute intervals with 5-minute breaks in between. After completing four intervals, he would take a longer break of 15-30 minutes. This new approach allowed Wyatt to maintain his focus during work periods while giving his mind and body the necessary time to recharge.

As Wyatt continued to integrate breaks into his daily routine, he noticed a significant improvement in his productivity and overall mental clarity. He no longer felt guilty or anxious about taking time off, understanding that breaks were essential for maintaining his well-being and preventing burnout. Wyatt also found that his job satisfaction increased, as he was able to better manage stress and maintain a healthy work-life balance.

In the end, Wyatt's experience demonstrated the importance of challenging the belief that taking breaks is counterproductive. By incorporating regular breaks into his daily routine, Wyatt was able to foster a healthier work-life balance, improve his focus, and ultimately achieve higher levels of productivity. He now encourages his colleagues to prioritize breaks and recognize their value in maintaining long-term success.

Understanding why breaks are vital is the first step in overcoming feelings of guilt or anxiety associated with taking time off. Breaks help to prevent burnout, improve mental clarity, and enhance overall well-being. By integrating regular breaks into our work routines, we'll be better equipped to manage stress, maintain focus, and ultimately achieve higher levels of productivity.

It is essential for us to challenge the mindset that taking breaks is counterproductive. Breaks offer numerous benefits for mental and physical health and can significantly improve work performance. By incorporating regular breaks into our daily routines and overcoming feelings of guilt or anxiety, we'll foster a healthier work-life balance and set ourselves up for long-term success.

Time Slots of Tranquility

Setting healthy work boundaries is crucial for maintaining a balanced and productive professional life. One effective way to achieve this is by incorporating built-in breaks into your daily routine. Not only do these breaks help you refuel physically, but they also contribute significantly to your mental well-being. In fact, by stepping away from your tasks, you allow your mind to recharge, which in turn can improve your focus and productivity when you return to work.

The first step towards establishing work boundaries is to prioritize your lunch break. Taking this time for yourself is essential not only for nourishing your body but also for providing a much-needed mental respite. Indeed, a quality lunch break can help you relieve stress and prevent feelings of burnout. To ensure you take your lunch break consistently, schedule it in your digital calendar. By doing so, you create a designated window for your meal break and communicate to your colleagues that you are unavailable during that time, preventing potential scheduling conflicts.

In addition to scheduling your lunch break, it's important to block off other types of breaks throughout the day using your digital calendar. These breaks might include a quick walk or exercise session to stimulate blood circulation and reenergize your body, stretching breaks to alleviate muscle tension and reduce the risk of discomfort or injury, and brief moments for deep breathing or meditation, which can help lower stress levels and increase mental clarity. By integrating these breaks into your daily routine, you create opportunities for mental and physical recovery, ultimately promoting a healthier work-life balance.

Creating built-in breaks is an effective strategy for establishing work boundaries; however, it is essential to remain committed to these scheduled breaks. Consistency is key, as it helps develop a routine that supports your well-being and fosters a sustainable work environment.

Consider Doug, a dedicated high school teacher who often found himself overwhelmed by the demands of his profession. Grading papers, preparing lesson plans, and addressing students' concerns left him with little time for himself. Doug recognized the importance of setting healthy work boundaries to maintain a balanced and productive professional life.

To establish these boundaries, Doug decided to prioritize his lunch break. He made a conscious effort to step away from his desk and enjoy his meal in the staff room. This experience not only helped nourish his body but also provided a much-needed mental respite. As a result, Doug found that a quality lunch break allowed him to relieve stress and prevent feelings of burnout.

Doug also scheduled his lunch break in his digital calendar to ensure consistency. By blocking off that time each day, he created a designated window for his meal break and communicated his unavailability to his colleagues, avoiding potential scheduling conflicts.

Furthermore, Doug incorporated other types of breaks throughout his day. He took quick walks around the school campus during his free periods to reenergize and stretched in between classes to alleviate muscle tension. He even set aside brief moments for deep breathing exercises or meditation in his classroom, which helped lower his stress levels and increase mental clarity.

By integrating these breaks into his daily routine, Doug created opportunities for mental and physical recovery, promoting a healthier work-life balance. As he remained committed to these scheduled breaks, he developed a routine that supported his well-being and fostered a sustainable work environment.

Incorporating built-in breaks into your daily routine is a valuable tool for setting healthy work boundaries. By using your digital calendar to schedule and prioritize these breaks, you ensure that you take the necessary time to recharge, ultimately maintaining focus, productivity, and a balanced professional life.

Embracing the Power Down Mindset

Technology has become an omnipresent force that permeates nearly every facet of our daily lives, making it increasingly challenging to disengage from our devices and the relentless barrage of information they provide. One of the most essential boundaries you can create is the demarcation between work and personal life. However, this boundary is often blurred, with recent research suggesting that the average workday is extended by nearly 49 minutes due to technology (Perlow, 2017).

To safeguard a healthy work-life balance and stave off burnout, it is crucial for you to institute a firm deadline for the conclusion of your workday and adhere to it consistently. This requires not only physically distancing yourself from your workspace but also powering down your devices and disconnecting from digital platforms for the evening. Such boundaries can be difficult to implement, particularly if you are perpetually connected and always "on." Yet, it is essential to acknowledge that dedicating time to disconnect from work is not only vital for your mental and physical well-being but can also foster heightened productivity and creativity (Vorderer, Klimmt, & Ritterfeld, 2004).

Taking deliberate breaks from technology and disconnecting from work has been shown to yield numerous benefits for you. Research indicates that unplugging from work-related activities can lead to improved sleep quality, reduced stress levels, and enhanced cognitive function (Banks et al., 2010). Moreover, disconnecting from work can foster stronger relationships with family and friends, as it allows you to be fully present and engaged during personal interactions (Turkle, 2015). Additionally, periods of disconnection have been linked to increased creativity, as your mind is free to wander and explore novel ideas in the absence of constant stimulation (Zomorodi, 2015).

Parker was a hardworking project manager at a thriving technology company. Her days were filled with meetings, emails, and deadlines, and she often found herself working late into the night. Her dedication to her job was admirable, but it came at a significant cost to her personal life and well-being. She was constantly connected to her devices, answering work emails at all hours and even checking in on projects while spending time with her family.

Parker's persistent "always on" mentality began taking a toll on her health and relationships. She noticed her sleep quality deteriorating, her stress levels rising, and her once-fruitful creative ideas dwindling. Conversations with her spouse and friends were frequently interrupted by the incessant buzzing of her phone, leaving them feeling unheard and unimportant. It became increasingly evident to Parker that she needed to establish boundaries between her work and personal life to regain balance and protect her well-being.

Determined to make a change, Parker decided to institute a firm deadline for the end of her workday, vowing to adhere to it consistently. She chose 5 PM as her cut-off time, allowing for a reasonable buffer after the typical close of business. Parker informed her colleagues of her new boundary, requesting that they respect her disconnection time and avoid sending non-urgent work-related messages during the evening.

At first, the transition was challenging for Parker. The urge to check her email or respond to a text was strong, and the fear of missing out on important updates haunted her. However, she remained steadfast in her commitment to powering down her devices and disconnecting from digital platforms each evening.

Over time, Parker began to notice the benefits of her new boundary. Her sleep quality improved, her stress levels decreased, and she started to experience a resurgence of creativity. Free from the constant barrage of work-related information, her mind was able to wander and explore novel ideas during her downtime.

Furthermore, Parker's relationships with her spouse, children, and friends began to flourish. With her devices powered down, she was able to be fully present and engaged during personal interactions. She found renewed joy in simple pleasures like family dinners, movie nights, and weekend outings, realizing the importance of nurturing these connections.

As Parker continued to honor her work-life boundary, she also observed an increase in productivity during her work hours. By allowing herself the time to recharge and rejuvenate, she was better equipped to tackle projects and meet deadlines with renewed vigor and enthusiasm.

Parker's story serves as a powerful reminder of the importance of powering down technology and creating a healthy work-life balance. By setting a firm deadline for the end of the workday and disconnecting from digital platforms, you can safeguard your mental and physical well-being, foster stronger relationships, and unleash your full creative potential.

In light of these considerations, the next time you feel tempted to send just one more email or peruse your work messages before turning in for the night, remember the importance of powering down and affording yourself the rest and relaxation you deserve. Choose a specific time to wrap up your workday and remain steadfast in your commitment to disconnect, switching off your devices for the night. Your mind and body will undoubtedly appreciate the reprieve.

Mastering the Art of Powering Down Technology

In the fast-paced and interconnected world we live in, technology has made it increasingly challenging to separate work from personal life. The constant tug-of-war between the two can lead to burnout, stress, and a diminished sense of well-being. To maintain a healthy work-life balance, it is essential to disconnect from technology and create a more fulfilling life. In this article, we will explore 12 practical strategies that can help you take control of your relationship with technology and achieve a harmonious work-life balance.

1. Disconnect from all electronic devices: Shut down your computer, phone, tablet, and any other work-related electronic devices. This conscious effort helps you disengage from work and shift your focus to other aspects of your life.

2. Establish boundaries: Determine a specific time each day when you will cease using technology for work purposes. This clearly delineates work and personal time, promoting a healthier balance.

3. Utilize website-blocking apps: Several applications and programs can restrict access to certain websites or apps during designated hours. By using these tools, you can prevent yourself from checking work-related emails or messages outside of work hours.

4. Take a social media hiatus: Social media can be a significant distraction, particularly concerning work. Dedicate a few hours each day to disengage from social media, which can help you detach from work.

5. Set alarms or reminders: Program an alarm or reminder to signal the end of the workday, serving as a prompt to power down technology and shift your focus elsewhere.

6. Organize your day with a journal or planner: Before disconnecting, spend a few minutes planning for the next day. This strategy clears your mind and allows you to unwind without fretting over work obligations.

7. Pursue alternative activities: Engage in leisurely activities that you enjoy after work, such as reading, exercising, or spending quality time with loved ones. These pursuits help you detach from work and concentrate on other meaningful aspects of life.

8. Disable notifications: Silence notifications for work-related apps or emails during non-work hours, eliminating the incessant distractions and enabling you to focus on personal time.

9. Take an email break: Refrain from checking work emails after hours, allowing you to disconnect from work and concentrate on other matters.

10. Activate "Do Not Disturb" mode: Set your phone to "Do Not Disturb" during non-work hours to avoid disruptions from work-related calls or text messages.

11. Practice meditation or mindfulness: Allocate a few minutes at the end of the day for meditation or mindfulness exercises. These techniques help clear your mind, focus on the present moment, and facilitate relaxation and disconnection from work.

12. Designate a work-free zone: Designate a specific area in your home where work-related technology use is off-limits. This physical boundary reinforces the separation between work and personal time.

By incorporating these twelve strategies into your daily routine, you can effectively power down technology and establish boundaries between your work and personal life. Strive for consistency in your approach and prioritize self-care to recharge and boost productivity in the long run. It is vital to remember that technology should be at your service, not vice versa. By gaining mastery over your relationship with technology, you are well on your way to enjoying a more balanced and fulfilling life.

Discovering the Power of Silence

It has become increasingly difficult to separate our work and personal lives. The constant barrage of notifications, messages, and emails can make it challenging to disconnect from work when we need to focus on our personal lives. By silencing notifications and establishing a schedule for checking and responding to work-related communication, we can effectively create the separation we need to thrive in both aspects of our lives.

One way to set boundaries with work is to not let it interfere with your personal time. This can be achieved by silencing notifications at the end of the day so that emails and messages aren't interrupting your dinner or family time. This will allow you to disconnect from work and fully focus on your personal life outside of the office. A study conducted by Virginia Tech in 2018 found that the mere expectation of being available for work after hours is linked to increased stress and anxiety, affecting not just the employee but their family as well (Park, Fritz, & Jex, 2018). By silencing notifications, we can reduce this stress and enjoy our personal time more fully.

In addition to silencing notifications, you can also set specific hours for checking and responding to work emails and messages. For example, you could designate a certain time in the morning and afternoon for checking and responding to emails, and then turn off your work email at the end of the day. This will help you to stay focused and avoid getting pulled into work outside of your designated work hours. In a study conducted by the University of British Columbia, participants who limited their email checking to three times a day reported lower stress levels and increased feelings of well-being (Kushlev & Dunn, 2015).

The importance of setting boundaries between work and personal life cannot be overstated. When we fail to establish these boundaries, we risk burnout, decreased productivity, and strained relationships with our loved ones. According to the American Psychological Association, chronic work stress can lead to serious mental health issues, such as depression and anxiety, and physical health problems, like hypertension and heart disease (American Psychological Association, 2021).

An example of someone who successfully set boundaries is Harper, a marketing manager in a busy tech company, the line between work and personal life had become increasingly blurred. The never-ending stream of notifications, messages, and emails made it nearly impossible for her to disconnect from work when she needed to focus on her family and personal well-being. Harper knew that she needed to set boundaries to maintain a healthy work-life balance and protect her mental and physical health.

To do so, Harper began by silencing her notifications after her work hours, ensuring that work emails and messages wouldn't interrupt her evenings with her family. This simple act allowed her to disconnect from work and fully immerse herself in her personal life. Harper noticed that her stress levels decreased, and she could enjoy her time with her family without the constant pressure of being available for work.

Furthermore, Harper decided to allocate specific hours during the day for checking and responding to work emails and messages. She designated a certain time in the morning and afternoon for this task and turned off her work email at the end of the day. This practice helped her stay focused on her personal life outside of work and avoid getting pulled back into work-related matters during her personal time. As a result, Harper experienced lower stress levels and a greater sense of well-being, just like the participants in the University of British Columbia study (Kushlev & Dunn, 2015).

By setting clear boundaries between work and personal life, Harper managed to avoid the detrimental effects of failing to do so, such as burnout, decreased productivity, and strained relationships. She also protected herself from the serious mental and physical health issues linked to chronic work stress, as highlighted by the American Psychological Association (2021).

In the end, Harper's commitment to setting boundaries between her work and personal life allowed her to maintain her mental and physical health, while still excelling in her professional life. She learned the importance of nurturing her personal life, and her newfound balance made her more successful both at work and at home.

It is essential to set boundaries between work and personal life to maintain our mental and physical health. By silencing notifications and establishing a schedule for checking and responding to work-related communication, we can create a healthy balance that allows us to thrive both personally and professionally. The consequences of not setting these boundaries can be severe, leading to burnout, decreased productivity, and strained relationships. As we strive for success in our careers, it's crucial not to forget the importance of nurturing our personal lives as well.

The Transformative Power of Routines

Routines play a crucial role in our lives, offering a wide range of benefits that contribute to personal and professional success. Understanding their transformative power can help us lead more organized, focused, and fulfilling lives.

First and foremost, routines impart a sense of structure and order, cultivating feelings of security and stability. This foundation proves particularly beneficial during periods of change, transition, or uncertainty, providing a reassuring anchor amidst the chaos. Furthermore, routines enhance productivity and efficiency by presenting a well-defined plan of action. This roadmap eliminates guesswork, reduces distractions, and keeps us on track, ensuring that we achieve our goals in a timely and organized manner. The predictability and control offered by routines serve as potent stress and anxiety reducers, helping us maintain emotional and mental well-being.

By incorporating regular habits into our daily lives, we can minimize the burden of decision-making, thus mitigating mental fatigue. This streamlining of choices allows us to dedicate more energy and focus to the tasks at hand, fostering a sense of accomplishment and satisfaction.

One key aspect of creating effective routines is integrating transitional activities that mentally separate professional and personal time. For instance, a 15-minute journaling session before work can stimulate the mind, mentally preparing us for the day's challenges. Conversely, a 30-minute post-work workout can dissipate stress and tension, promoting relaxation and a smooth transition into personal time.

Sebastian, a 35-year-old physician at a busy metropolitan hospital, has always struggled with maintaining a work-life balance. His demanding schedule and intense workload often leave little time for personal pursuits and self-care. Upon discovering the transformative power of routines, he decides to make significant changes in his life to lead a more organized, focused, and fulfilling life.

To start, Sebastian establishes a morning routine to create a sense of structure and order in his life. He wakes up at 5:00 am every day, allowing himself time for a nutritious breakfast and a 15-minute meditation session. This practice not only helps him mentally prepare for the day ahead but also sets a positive tone for the day.

At the hospital, Sebastian implements a routine to enhance productivity and efficiency. He begins each day by reviewing his patient list and organizing them by priority. He allocates specific time slots for rounds, consultations, and administrative tasks, ensuring that he remains focused and on track. This well-defined plan of action eliminates guesswork, reduces distractions, and instills a sense of predictability and control over his workday.

To further streamline his day and minimize decision-making, Sebastian adopts a weekly meal planning strategy. He dedicates time on Sundays to plan his meals and grocery shop, allowing him to quickly prepare healthy and balanced meals throughout the week without expending unnecessary mental energy.

Sebastian recognizes the importance of integrating transitional activities into his routine to separate his professional and personal time. After completing his hospital duties, he commits to a 30-minute workout, which helps him dissipate stress and tension while promoting relaxation. This activity also serves as a mental boundary, signaling to his mind that work is over and personal time has begun.

To foster healthy habits, Sebastian incorporates regular exercise, balanced meals, and quality sleep into his daily routine. He makes it a point to get at least 7 hours of sleep every night and participates in a local cycling club twice a week. These activities contribute to noticeable improvements in his physical and mental well-being.

Periodically, Sebastian evaluates and adjusts his routines to align with his evolving needs and priorities. He remains flexible and open to change, ensuring that his routines continue to support both his personal and professional growth.

Through the implementation of daily routines, Sebastian experiences a dramatic transformation in his life. He now enjoys optimized time management, prioritized responsibilities, and increased focus on the aspects that matter most to him. By harnessing the transformative power of routines, Sebastian paves the way for a more organized, balanced, and fulfilling life as a dedicated physician.

Consistently engaging in such transitional activities establishes a sense of routine and structure, facilitating a seamless shift between different life domains. In essence, routines function as our default behavior, setting mental boundaries and nurturing a sense of normalcy and predictability.

Additionally, routines can foster healthy habits, which contribute to our overall well-being. By incorporating activities such as regular exercise, balanced meals, and quality sleep into our daily routines, we can experience tangible improvements in our physical and mental health. Over time, these habits become ingrained, making it easier to maintain a lifestyle that promotes wellness and longevity.

To further enhance the effectiveness of our routines, it's important to periodically evaluate and adjust them to suit our evolving needs and priorities. By remaining flexible and open to change, we can ensure that our routines continue to support our personal and professional growth.

Embracing a daily routine enables us to optimize time management, prioritize responsibilities, and maintain focus on the aspects that matter most in our lives. By harnessing the transformative power of routines, we can pave the way for a more organized, balanced, and fulfilling existence.

Self-Assessment - Managing Technology and Work Boundaries

Managing technology and establishing healthy work boundaries are imperative to ensuring a balanced and productive life. This self-assessment is designed to provide a reflection on how well you are managing your technological involvement and defining your professional boundaries. The ensuing questions offer a nuanced exploration of these elements, encouraging a mindful approach to your work-life balance.

For each question, rate yourself on a scale of 1 to 5, where 1 is "strongly disagree" and 5 is "strongly agree."

1. I have clearly defined non-negotiables when it comes to work.
2. I regularly prioritize my tasks, focusing on what is most important and urgent.
3. I frequently review my job description to ensure alignment with my priorities and boundaries.
4. I am comfortable delegating tasks to maintain a manageable workload.
5. I take time to respond thoughtfully to emails and messages, rather than reacting impulsively.
6. I can take time off without feeling guilty or overwhelmed.
7. I create built-in breaks throughout my workday to recharge and refocus.
8. I regularly disconnect from technology to maintain a healthy work-life balance.
9. I silence notifications and establish a schedule to help maintain my work boundaries.
10. I have incorporated routines into my daily life, leading to improved overall well-being and work boundaries.
11. I effectively manage my workload by focusing on my top priorities.
12. I communicate my work and technology boundaries to my coworkers and supervisors.
13. I can set boundaries with technology, even during busy periods or high-stress situations.
14. I feel in control of my technology use, rather than letting it control me.
15. I have successfully established a routine that allows for work, personal time, and disconnection from technology.
16. I recognize when technology is negatively impacting my work-life

balance and take action to correct it.

17. I have a designated time and space for using technology to maintain work boundaries.

18. I actively seek ways to improve my work-life balance through better management of technology and work boundaries.

19. I have a healthy relationship with technology, using it as a tool to enhance my work and personal life, rather than letting it consume me.

20. I regularly reassess my technology and work boundaries to ensure they are effective and in line with my values and goals.

Interpretation

To evaluate your results on this self-assessment, add up your total score and use the following scale:

Total Score: 20-40

Room for Improvement: Your score suggests that you may have significant challenges managing technology and work boundaries. Reflect on the areas where you scored lower and consider implementing new strategies or routines to improve your work-life balance and relationship with technology.

Total Score: 41-60

Making Progress: Your score indicates that you have taken some steps to manage your technology and work boundaries, but there is still room for improvement. Analyze the areas where you scored lower and think about how you can enhance your work-life balance by refining your boundaries.

Total Score: 61-80

Balanced Approach: Your score suggests that you have a fairly balanced approach to managing technology and work boundaries. Continue to reflect on and refine your boundaries as needed, and consider sharing your successful strategies with others who may be struggling.

Total Score: 81-100

Excellent Management: Your score indicates that you are effectively managing your technology and work boundaries, leading to a healthy work-life balance. Keep up the great work, and continue to reassess your boundaries as your circumstances change.

This assessment serves as a tool for introspection, shedding light on the way you manage technology and your work boundaries. Continually reassessing these aspects is key to ensuring that they remain effective, aligned with your values and goals, and conducive to a healthy work-life balance. Remember, the power to manage technology and work boundaries lies in your hands and shapes your overall well-being and productivity.

Exercise: Managing Technology and Work Boundaries

1. What are three aspects of your work that you consider absolutely non-negotiable, and why? Reflect on a time you compromised on these. What were the consequences?
2. How have your priorities aligned with your work/life balance? Can you identify any misalignments and outline steps to better align your priorities?
3. How well does your actual day-to-day work align with your official job description? Are there tasks you consistently perform that fall outside your role? How might addressing this improve your work boundaries?
4. Can you identify a task you've been performing that could be more efficiently handled by someone else? What has been preventing you from delegating this task, and how can you overcome that?
5. Have you ever felt pressured to respond immediately to a work-related issue outside of your working hours? How did that impact your personal time, and how can you better manage such situations in the future?
6. How often do you plan time off, and how do you ensure that your work does not encroach upon this time? Can you identify ways to improve this process?
7. Reflect on your break habits during your workday. Do you consistently take sufficient breaks, or do you often work through

them? How might taking regular, scheduled breaks improve your productivity and work-life balance?

8. How often do you fully disconnect from work-related technology outside of your working hours? How does this affect your personal life, and what changes could you implement to improve this balance?

9. Can you recall a situation at work where taking a moment of silence before responding would have resulted in a better outcome? How can you integrate moments of silence into your daily routine?

10. Reflect on your current daily routine. Are there any changes you can make to better separate your work time from your personal time?

11. Can you think of a situation where saying 'no' would have better protected your boundaries? What prevented you from doing so and how can you overcome this in the future?

12. How do you incorporate self-care into your daily routine? How does this impact your ability to maintain healthy boundaries at work, and how can you improve in this area?

Chapter 6: Communicating Your Boundaries

"Boundaries teach others how to treat us by showing them what we will and will not accept." – Mark Groves

Laying the Foundation

Boundaries operate as the unseen thresholds that encapsulate our personal universe, encompassing both the physical and the intangible aspects of our lives. They are pivotal in molding our sense of identity, drawing the contours of the psychological landscape we consider our own. Setting boundaries serves as more than just a means of defining our territory; it also serves as a powerful declaration of our uniqueness and individuality. It lays the foundation for a self-concept that is shaped by our understanding of who we are and how we choose to engage with the world around us.

By setting robust boundaries, we exercise a degree of control over our environment, cultivating a framework that structures our interactions with others. This control acts as a safeguard, a wall that protects our emotional and mental health. It ensures that our personal space is respected and that our internal sanctum is protected. Nevertheless, this process isn't one-sided; it is a dynamic interplay that necessitates effective communication with the other players in our lives.

Communicating your boundaries is as vital as establishing them. If boundaries are the walls of our metaphorical home, communication is the gate that allows selective entrance. This calls for assertive communication, a fundamental tool in expressing our boundaries. It is not a display of dominance, but rather a clear, respectful conveyance of our expectations and limitations. It serves as a guide to others, outlining what behaviors we deem acceptable and which ones we consider intrusive.

However, it's important to remember that not everyone may be receptive to your boundaries. This could be due to differing perspectives or unfamiliarity with the concept of respecting personal boundaries. Resistance or pushback is not uncommon, but this should not deter you from upholding your limits. It is in these moments that our commitment to our boundaries is tested, reinforcing the importance of assertive communication and the courage to stand our ground.

The ability to say "no" is a crucial skill in maintaining boundaries. It is a firm declaration of our limits and a refusal to permit any encroachments. While it may be viewed as negative or confrontational, saying "no" is a significant act of self-preservation. It emphasizes that our well-being is a priority and that we have the right to control our interactions.

Yet, maintaining boundaries need not be an aggressive or confrontational act. In fact, it is more productive to create a non-confrontational atmosphere conducive to understanding and empathy. This begins with recognizing that everyone has their unique set of boundaries, crafted by their experiences and perspectives. Expressing our boundaries while acknowledging and respecting those of others establishes a mutual understanding, fostering a healthy environment where empathy thrives.

Boundaries are an integral part of our identity and mental well-being. They empower us with control over our environment and serve as a shield, protecting our emotional space. Effective and assertive communication is key in expressing these boundaries, and the ability to say "no" is a vital tool in upholding them. Despite potential resistance, we must remember that our well-being is paramount and deserves respect. By fostering a non-confrontational atmosphere of understanding and empathy, we can ensure that our boundaries are not only established but also respected, paving the way for healthier and more fulfilling relationships.

Prepare For Pushback

People often resist boundaries because they perceive them as a restriction on their freedom or a challenge to their established behavior patterns. In many cases, people have become accustomed to a certain level of flexibility or control in their relationships, and the introduction of boundaries can feel like an unwelcome change. They may interpret the establishment of boundaries as a sign of rejection or a personal attack, even if the intention behind the boundaries is to promote healthier interactions and mutual respect. Furthermore, some people may view boundaries as an attempt to impose one's will on them, which can trigger feelings of resentment and resistance.

Another reason people might dislike boundaries being set on them is the fear of being perceived as less valuable or less influential in a relationship or a group dynamic. Boundaries can challenge the status quo and disrupt the power balance in relationships, causing those who previously enjoyed a certain level of authority or control to feel threatened. They may worry that their position, importance, or even their sense of self is being diminished, leading to a negative emotional response. It is crucial to understand that while setting boundaries may be uncomfortable at first, the ultimate goal is to foster healthier, more balanced relationships that prioritize self-care and respect for one another.

As you begin to establish healthy boundaries, be prepared for pushback from your coworkers and clients. This is normal and can actually be a sign that the boundaries you're setting are necessary and effective. When we set boundaries, we are essentially saying that there are certain things that we will not tolerate in our relationships. This can be difficult for others to accept, especially if they are used to taking advantage of our willingness to put up with disrespectful or inappropriate behaviour. However, it's important to remember that establishing boundaries is not about being mean or trying to control others. It's about taking care of ourselves and making sure that we are treated with the respect and consideration that we deserve.

One way to prepare for pushback is to visualize scenarios where your boundaries are crossed. This can help you to identify potential triggers and practice responding in a calm and rational way. For example, let's say that you've decided that you will no longer work late on evenings and weekends. If a colleague asks you to stay late to finish a project, you could imagine yourself saying something like, "I'm sorry, but I'm not available to work late tonight. I have a personal commitment that I need to honour." By visualizing this situation in advance, you can prepare yourself to handle it in a confident and assertive way when it actually occurs. This can help you to stay calm and avoid getting emotional or defensive, which can make the situation worse. In addition to preparing for pushback, it's also helpful to have a support system in place. This could be a trusted colleague, friend, or family member who can offer you encouragement and advice when you're facing challenges at work. Having someone to talk to can help you to stay focused and motivated as you work to establish and maintain your boundaries. It can also provide you with a sounding board for ideas and strategies that can help you to effectively navigate difficult situations. Pushback is a normal and expected part of the process of establishing healthy boundaries.

Meet Mark. He's been working at a marketing firm for a year and has been doing his best to be a team player, even if it means taking on extra tasks or working long hours. However, lately he's been feeling burnt out and stressed, and he realizes that he needs to set some boundaries in order to take better care of himself. Mark starts by identifying the areas in his job that are causing him the most stress. He realizes that he's been working overtime almost every day and has been sacrificing his personal time in order to meet deadlines. He also notices that some of his colleagues have been taking advantage of his willingness to help and have been passing on their work to him.

Mark decides that he needs to start saying "no" to requests that are not within his job responsibilities and establish clear boundaries around his work hours. He has a conversation with his manager and explains that while he's happy to help out with urgent matters, he won't be able to continue working overtime on a regular basis. He also speaks with his colleagues and lets them know that he's not available to take on additional work that falls outside of his job description. At first, Mark's colleagues don't take him seriously and push back against his new boundaries. However, Mark remains firm and communicates his boundaries in a calm and assertive manner. He even visualizes scenarios where his boundaries may be crossed and practices responding in a confident and rational way.

With time, Mark's colleagues begin to respect his boundaries and he starts to feel more in control of his work and personal life. He even notices that his productivity and creativity have improved as a result of taking better care of himself. By setting healthy boundaries, Mark has learned to prioritize his needs and is enjoying a healthier and more fulfilling work life.

Setting healthy boundaries is an essential aspect of taking care of oneself, especially in the workplace. It is normal to experience pushback from colleagues when setting boundaries, but it is important to remain firm and communicate them in a calm and assertive manner. Visualizing potential scenarios and having a support system in place can help to navigate difficult situations effectively. By setting and maintaining boundaries, we can prioritize our needs and improve our work and personal lives. Mark's experience is an example of how setting healthy boundaries can lead to a healthier and more fulfilling work life.

Asserting Your Rights

Many of us may feel that we do not have the right to set boundaries, but this is not true. Setting boundaries is an important part of maintaining a healthy and productive work environment because it allows us to communicate our needs and expectations to our coworkers and clients, which can lead to a more positive and respectful work culture.

Asserting your rights involves recognizing your personal and professional value, and being willing to communicate your needs and boundaries with confidence. When you assert your rights, you're not only advocating for yourself, but also setting an example for others, empowering them to stand up for their own needs and creating a more balanced and supportive work environment. By asserting your rights, you contribute to fostering a work culture where everyone's needs are acknowledged and respected, ultimately leading to a more productive and harmonious atmosphere.

Setting boundaries does not mean being rude or uncooperative, but rather it is about creating clear lines of communication and respecting the boundaries of others. It is essential for our own well-being and the well-being of those around us to set boundaries. It's important to remember that standing up for ourselves and setting healthy boundaries at work is not only a healthy and necessary part of any professional relationship, but it is also a fundamental right.

Every person has the right to assert their own needs and boundaries, and to be treated with respect and dignity. This includes the right to say no to unreasonable demands or requests, to set limits on what we are comfortable with, and to have our boundaries respected by others. Standing up for ourselves can be difficult, especially if we've been socialized to prioritize the needs of others over our own.

Amy is a software developer at a fast-paced startup. She loves her job, but lately, she's been feeling overwhelmed and overworked. Her manager has been assigning her more and more projects, and she's struggling to keep up with the workload.

One day, her manager comes to her with yet another project, asking her to work overtime to complete it. Amy knows that she's already stretched thin and can't take on any more work, so she decides to assert her boundaries and rights.

She calmly tells her manager that she's unable to take on the project and that she needs to prioritize her current workload to ensure that she delivers high-quality work. She also reminds him that she's working within her agreed-upon working hours and that she cannot work overtime without prior notice.

Her manager initially seems disappointed, but he ultimately respects her decision and agrees to assign the project to another team member. Amy feels proud of herself for standing up for her needs and boundaries and knows that this is an important step towards maintaining a healthy work-life balance.

It's important to remember that we have a right to assert ourselves and to have our boundaries respected. So if you're feeling guilty for standing up for yourself, try to reframe the situation and remind yourself that you have a right to your own needs and feelings, and that it's okay to assert yourself and set healthy boundaries in order to take care of yourself.

Understanding Your Rights at Work

All human beings are entitled to their human rights.

Every person has certain inalienable rights that are essential for their personal growth, safety, and wellbeing. These rights empower you to make choices that align with your values and beliefs, stand up for yourself when you feel disrespected or undervalued, and pursue your dreams and aspirations with confidence. However, you may not be fully aware of your rights, or you may feel guilty or selfish when exercising them. This can lead to feelings of dissatisfaction, frustration, and resentment, which can negatively impact your mental and emotional health. Therefore, it's crucial to recognize and honor your rights as an individual to live a fulfilling and meaningful life.

Here is a list of your rights:

1. I have the right to say no.
2. I have the right to be wrong.
3. I have the right to be my True Self.
4. I have the right to change my mind at any time.
5. I have the right to make mistakes and learn from them.
6. I have the right to ask for what I want.
7. I have the right to be treated with dignity and respect.
8. I have the right to be treated fairly and with respect.
9. I have the right to a safe and healthy work environment.
10. I have the right to take breaks and have time for rest and recovery.
11. I have the right to be paid at least the minimum wage.
12. I have the right to form or join a union.
13. I have the right to negotiate for change.
14. I have the right to reject unsolicited advice or feedback.
15. I have the right to privacy and personal space.
16. I have the right to detach from anyone in whose company I feel humiliated or manipulated.
17. I have the right to refuse to take responsibility for anyone else's problems.
18. I have the right to be treated with respect and dignity by

coworkers, supervisors, and clients.

19. I have the right to expect that others will not behave in a disrespectful or abusive manner towards me.

20. I have the right to set boundaries around time and energy.

21. I have the right to be free from retaliation or punishment for asserting rights or setting boundaries in the workplace.

22. I have the right to fair compensation and benefits, and to expect to be paid.

23. I have the right to a fair and just grievance process for addressing and resolving workplace conflicts and issues.

24. I have the right to reasonable accommodations for disabilities or religious beliefs.

25. I have the right to a fair and transparent promotion and advancement process.

26. I have the right to be informed of company policies and procedures.

27. I have the right to a work-life balance and to not be overworked or expected to work excessive hours without fair compensation.

28. I have the right to a clear and detailed job description and expectations.

29. I have the right to live life happy, joyous, and free.

30. I have a right to grow, evolve and prosper.

31. I have the right to be acknowledged and recognized for my accomplishments and contributions.

32. I have the right to equal opportunities for career growth and development regardless of my gender, race, religion, or other protected characteristics.

33. I have the right to access resources and support to perform my job effectively and efficiently.

34. I have the right to clear and open communication with my supervisors, colleagues, and clients.

35. I have the right to express my opinions and ideas in a respectful and constructive manner.

36. I have the right to a workplace that supports my mental and emotional well-being.

37. I have the right to periodic performance evaluations and constructive feedback.

38. I have the right to be protected from workplace bullying and harassment.

39. I have the right to a transparent and unbiased recruitment process.

40. I have the right to reasonable job security and protection from unfair dismissal.

41. I have the right to access professional development opportunities and training to enhance my skills and knowledge.

42. I have the right to a workplace culture that fosters inclusivity and diversity.

43. I have the right to flexible work arrangements to accommodate personal needs and responsibilities.

44. I have the right to a reasonable and fair workload that is commensurate with my role and capabilities.

45. I have the right to be consulted on decisions that significantly impact my job and work environment.

46. I have the right to maintain a healthy separation between my personal and professional life.

47. I have the right to be treated with empathy and understanding during difficult personal circumstances.

48. I have the right to seek assistance and support from my employer for issues affecting my job performance and overall well-being.

49. I have the right to take time off work for things like vacation, illness, and family emergencies.

50. I have the right to receive training and development opportunities to help me do my job better.

Exercising your rights is not a selfish act, but rather a necessary one to ensure your personal and professional growth and development. It's essential to know and understand your rights so that you can assert them when needed and create boundaries that respect your values and beliefs. By embracing your rights, you empower yourself to be true to who you are, pursue your goals with conviction, and contribute positively to the world around you.

Mastering the Art of Saying 'No'

Learning to say no is a skill that can have a significant impact on your overall well-being, productivity, and happiness. Saying no can be challenging, especially if you're used to saying yes to everything, but it's an essential skill to learn if you want to maintain healthy boundaries, prioritize your goals, and avoid becoming overwhelmed.

When you're constantly saying yes to others, you risk spreading yourself too thin and neglecting your own needs and priorities. You may find yourself taking on more than you can handle, feeling stressed and anxious, and struggling to keep up with your commitments. Saying no allows you to create space in your life for the things that truly matter to you.

"No is a complete sentence" is a powerful concept to remember when setting boundaries. It means that you have the right to decline a request or an invitation without feeling the need to provide an elaborate explanation. You are allowed to prioritize your needs and protect your time and energy. Understanding this concept can be liberating, as it gives you the freedom to make choices based on your values and goals, rather than being driven by guilt or the fear of disappointing others. While it's important to be respectful and considerate when saying no, it's equally important to recognize that you don't always have to justify your decision. Embracing the notion that "no is a complete sentence" can empower you to assert your boundaries with greater confidence and authenticity, leading to a more balanced and fulfilling life.

In order to learn to say no effectively, it's important to understand why you struggle to say no in the first place. For many people, saying no feels uncomfortable or even scary because they fear rejection or conflict. Others may feel guilty or selfish for saying no, or worry about what others will think of them. Identifying your personal barriers to saying no can help you overcome them and become more assertive in your communication. One way to practice saying no is to start small. You can begin by saying no to small requests or invitations, such as declining a social event that you're not interested in attending. Gradually, you can work your way up to saying no to bigger requests or obligations, such as turning down a work project that doesn't align with your goals or values.

When you do need to say no, it's important to do so in a clear, respectful, and assertive way. You can explain your reasons for declining the request or offer, but you don't need to justify or apologize for your decision. You can simply say something like, "I appreciate the offer, but I'm not able to commit to that at this time." In the workplace, saying no can be particularly challenging because you may feel pressure to say yes to your manager or colleagues. However, learning to say no in a professional and respectful way can actually increase your credibility and earn you respect from others. It's important to communicate your boundaries clearly and to suggest alternative solutions or compromises when possible.

Learning to say no is about taking charge of your time and energy and using them in a manner consistent with your values and goals. It's not about being selfish or uncooperative; it's about being assertive and effectively communicating your boundaries. You can reduce stress and overwhelm, prioritize your goals, and create a more fulfilling and balanced life by saying no when necessary. When you are faced with requests or obligations that do not align with your priorities, it is especially important to say no. This could include anything from invitations to social events that you have no interest in attending to extra work assignments. You may find yourself stretched too thin, with less time and energy to devote to the things that are most important to you when you agree to these requests.

By saying no, you make room in your life for the things you truly care about. You can focus on your personal and professional objectives, pursue hobbies and interests that bring you joy, and cultivate relationships with your loved ones. When you learn to say no, you become more deliberate with your time and energy, which enables you to live a more fulfilling and significant life. Learning to say no can also boost your confidence and sense of self-worth. When you communicate your boundaries with assertiveness, you demonstrate that you value your own needs and priorities. You can increase your self-awareness and self-respect, thereby enhancing your relationships with others and overall sense of well-being.

Imagine that your manager asks you to take on a new project that requires a significant amount of time and resources. However, you know that you're already working on several other projects that are equally important and will require a lot of your attention. In this situation, you can say no in a respectful and assertive way. You can start by expressing your appreciation for the opportunity and acknowledging the importance of the new project. Then, you can explain your reasons for declining the request. For example, you could say something like, "Thank you for considering me for this project. While I appreciate the opportunity, I don't think I can take it on at this time. I'm currently working on several other projects that are equally important and will require a lot of my attention. I want to make sure that I can give all of my projects the time and resources they deserve, and I don't want to compromise the quality of my work or risk burnout." You can then suggest alternative solutions or compromises, such as delegating some of the work to a colleague or re-prioritizing your existing projects to make room for the new one. By communicating your boundaries and proposing alternative solutions, you demonstrate your professionalism and commitment to your work while also protecting your well-being and managing your workload effectively.

According to a study published in the Journal of Personality and Social Psychology, setting boundaries and saying no can improve overall life satisfaction and psychological well-being. Participants in the study who reported being better at setting boundaries also reported higher levels of happiness and lower levels of negative emotions when compared to those who struggled to set boundaries. The study discovered that saying no can lead to increased productivity and better decision-making. The researchers discovered that people who had difficulty saying no were more likely to experience decision fatigue and make impulsive decisions. Those who could say no more easily, on the other hand, were able to conserve their mental resources and make more thoughtful and deliberate decisions.

Overall, research suggests that learning to say no can have numerous benefits, including improved well-being, productivity, and workplace satisfaction. By setting clear boundaries and communicating assertively, you can create a healthier and more fulfilling work and personal life.

The Art of Diplomatic Refusal

Learning how to say no politely and effectively is crucial for maintaining a healthy work-life balance, reducing stress, and avoiding burnout. However, many people find it challenging to decline requests from their colleagues, supervisors, or clients. There are several key strategies that can help make saying no easier and more effective.

First, it's important to understand when it's appropriate to say no. There may be times when you're already overloaded with tasks and simply cannot take on any more work without sacrificing quality or risking burnout. Alternatively, you may lack the necessary skills or resources to complete a task, or it may conflict with your personal values or goals. By recognizing these situations, you can make informed decisions about when to say no and when to take on additional responsibilities.

When communicating your decision to say no, it's important to choose the appropriate time and place to do so. Avoiding confrontational or stressful situations can help make the conversation more productive and respectful. Additionally, using polite and respectful language can help maintain positive relationships with colleagues, clients, or supervisors.

Offering alternative solutions can also be helpful in finding a middle ground that works for everyone involved. For example, you might suggest delegating the task to another colleague or revising the timeline or scope of the project. By working together to find a solution that meets everyone's needs, you can maintain positive working relationships and avoid conflicts.

If pushback or conflicts do arise, it's important to stay assertive and firm in your decision while also managing your emotions and staying calm. Finding common ground and resolving conflicts can help maintain positive working relationships and reduce stress and tension. This might involve setting limits and boundaries with colleagues, taking regular breaks throughout the workday, or prioritizing activities outside of work that bring you joy and fulfillment.

It's important to note that saying no at work can be particularly challenging for those who are new to a job or who have a more junior position within the organization. In these situations, there may be a fear of being seen as uncooperative or risking future opportunities for advancement. However, it's important to remember that saying no can actually demonstrate a level of professionalism and self-awareness that is highly valued in the workplace.

One helpful strategy for saying no is to frame your decision in terms of what you can do, rather than what you can't do. For example, instead of saying "I can't take on that project right now," you might say "I would be happy to help with that project once I've finished the tasks that are currently on my plate." This approach can help you maintain a positive and helpful attitude while still setting boundaries around your workload. It's also important to recognize that saying no can sometimes lead to unexpected opportunities. By turning down a task or project that isn't a good fit for your skills or goals, you may open up space for other, more fulfilling opportunities to arise. It can be helpful to reframe saying no as a way of making intentional choices about how you spend your time and energy, rather than as a negative or difficult experience.

Let's say you work in a team where your supervisor frequently assigns you tasks that are outside of your job description or require a significant amount of time and effort. You've already taken on several of these tasks and are feeling overwhelmed, so when your supervisor asks you to take on another one, you decide it's time to say no.

Instead of simply declining the request outright, you might approach the conversation by acknowledging your supervisor's needs and expressing your own limitations. For example, you might say something like: "Thanks for considering me for this project. I really appreciate the opportunity to contribute to the team. However, I have to be honest that I'm feeling a bit stretched right now. I have a few other high-priority tasks on my plate, and I'm worried that taking on this project might mean sacrificing the quality of my work or missing deadlines. Is there any way we could revisit the timeline for this project or find another colleague who might be better suited for the task?"

By framing your response in a way that acknowledges your supervisor's needs while also expressing your own limitations, you can demonstrate your professionalism and commitment to the team while still setting appropriate boundaries around your workload. Offering alternative solutions, such as revisiting the timeline or suggesting another colleague, can also help maintain positive relationships with your supervisor and colleagues while still prioritizing your own well-being.

Ultimately, learning how to say no at work is an ongoing process that requires practice and reflection. By understanding your own priorities, setting boundaries, and communicating your decisions respectfully and effectively, you can maintain positive relationships with colleagues and supervisors while also prioritizing your own well-being and achieving your goals.

Harnessing the Power of 'I' Messages in Communication

In any workplace setting, communication is essential, but it can be challenging to express our needs and wants without coming across as confrontational or aggressive. This is where the use of "I" messages can be beneficial. An "I" message allows us to express our feelings, needs, or wants in a way that avoids blame or criticism of others. This approach is particularly effective when setting boundaries. By being specific and concrete, we are more likely to get the support we need.

An "I" message is a statement that expresses our own feelings, needs, or wants, rather than placing blame or criticism on others. For example, instead of saying "You're always talking too loudly and it's disrupting my work," an "I" message would be "I need a quiet environment to focus on my work." The key difference between "I" messages and "you" messages is that "I" messages focus on our own feelings and needs, while "you" messages focus on the behavior of others. Using "I" messages in setting boundaries is an effective way to communicate our needs and wants in a clear and assertive manner. It's important to identify and express our needs and wants in a specific and concrete way. For example, instead of saying "I need more help," we could say "I need assistance with completing this project by the deadline." By being specific and concrete, we are more likely to get the support we need.

When setting boundaries with "I" messages, it's also important to communicate them clearly and assertively. This means being confident and firm in expressing our needs and wants, without being aggressive or confrontational. We should also be prepared for pushback or resistance from others, and be willing to negotiate and compromise if necessary. "I" messages can be used to set boundaries with coworkers and supervisors. For example, if a coworker is always talking too loudly and it's disrupting our work, we can assert our need for quiet during focused work by saying "I need a quiet environment to focus on my work." Another example is when we need to communicate our availability for overtime or additional projects to our supervisor, we can express our need for a healthy work-life balance by saying "I am happy to help, but I need to maintain a healthy work-life balance."

Let's say you're working on an important project and a coworker keeps interrupting you with questions and comments that are distracting you from your work. Instead of getting frustrated and snapping at them, you could use an "I" message to express your need for focus and concentration.

An example of an "I" message in this situation might be: "I'm feeling a bit overwhelmed with this project right now, and I need to be able to focus and concentrate to get it done on time. Could we set aside some time later today to go over any questions you have, so I can finish this work?"

By using an "I" message, you're expressing your own feelings and needs without placing blame or criticism on your coworker. You're also providing a specific solution that can help you both to get your work done efficiently. This approach is more likely to be well-received than if you were to lash out in frustration or make accusatory comments.

It's essential to note that setting boundaries using "I" messages takes practice and self-reflection. It's not always easy to express our needs and wants, especially with work. However, by being clear and assertive in expressing our needs and wants, we can create a healthier and more productive work environment. "I" messages are an effective way to set boundaries. They allow us to express our needs and wants in a clear and assertive manner while avoiding blame or criticism of others. It's essential to note that setting boundaries takes practice and self-reflection and it's important to encourage ongoing practice and self-reflection in setting boundaries.

Projecting Clarity and Confidence

Effective communication plays a pivotal role in establishing and maintaining healthy boundaries. It is vital to not only set boundaries, but to also convey them to those around us with clarity and confidence. This involves being specific about our needs and expectations.

One way to achieve this is by setting clear guidelines for when and how we can be contacted. For instance, explicitly stating our availability for work-related conversations allows our colleagues and employers to understand and respect our boundaries. To ensure clarity and consistency, it is essential to communicate these boundaries through emails or face-to-face conversations.

It is also crucial to define what constitutes an emergency, as this sets expectations and guidelines for when it is appropriate to contact or interact with someone. Establishing an emergency contact list can facilitate this understanding among our co-workers and clients.

Addressing boundary violations as soon as they occur is a key aspect of boundary setting. By reinforcing the importance of the boundary immediately after it has been breached, it sends a clear message that such behavior is unacceptable. Delaying this process may inadvertently convey that the violation is acceptable, making enforcement more difficult in the future.

Various practical methods can be employed to communicate boundaries effectively. A simple approach is to include a note in our email signature specifying the hours during which we will respond to emails and calls. This sets expectations for when others can reach us and helps us adhere to our boundaries.

It is crucial to recognize that communication is not a one-size-fits-all approach. As different people have unique communication styles and preferences, adapting our communication style to suit individual or group needs is essential. Whether it's face-to-face or written communication, expressing boundaries respectfully and assertively is vital. This allows us to communicate our needs and expectations confidently while considering the needs and expectations of others. Boundaries should not be about control or manipulation but respecting ourselves and our needs.

Self-awareness is a critical component of setting boundaries. Identifying our own needs and limitations enables us to communicate them effectively to others. Furthermore, being open to feedback and willing to make necessary adjustments helps cultivate stronger and healthier relationships.

Ethan, a project manager, understood the importance of setting boundaries and communicating them effectively to ensure a healthy work-life balance. He was specific about his needs and expectations, informing his team members that he would be available for work-related conversations from 9 AM to 5 PM on weekdays. He took the initiative to communicate this clearly through team meetings and follow-up emails, which allowed his colleagues to respect his boundaries.

In addition to setting his availability, Ethan defined what constituted an emergency and provided his team with an emergency contact list. This helped his team understand when it was appropriate to reach out to him outside of his stated working hours. He also made sure to address any boundary violations immediately, reinforcing the importance of respecting each other's boundaries. To further promote transparency, Ethan included a note in his email signature specifying his working hours and response time for emails and calls.

Ethan recognized that communication styles and preferences varied among his team members. He adapted his approach accordingly, ensuring that he expressed his boundaries respectfully and assertively. This not only allowed him to communicate his needs confidently but also took into account the needs and expectations of others. By being self-aware and open to feedback, Ethan was able to adjust his boundaries when necessary, fostering stronger and healthier relationships within his team. Ultimately, his clear and confident communication allowed him to maintain a balance between his professional and personal life.

It is essential to remember that boundaries are not set in stone and may need adjustments over time. Open and ongoing communication ensures that our boundaries remain effective and relevant.

Effective communication is the cornerstone of establishing and maintaining healthy boundaries. By being clear, specific, and respectful, we can meet our needs and strengthen our relationships. It is equally important to remain self-aware, open to feedback, and be willing to make adjustments when necessary. These skills empower us to establish healthy boundaries and foster strong, fulfilling relationships with others.

Strategies for Confident Boundary Communication

Establishing and maintaining healthy boundaries is an important aspect of self-care and healthy relationships. Communicating your boundaries effectively can be challenging, but using "I" statements, being specific, and addressing boundary violations immediately can help. By practicing boundary-setting techniques and reflecting on your needs and boundaries, you can establish a clear understanding of what is and is not acceptable behaviour in your relationships.

Here are some specific things you can do to communicate your boundaries clearly and confidently:

1. Use "I" statements: Express your feelings and needs using "I" statements, such as "I need quiet in order to focus" or "I am not comfortable with that". This communicates your boundaries in a non-confrontational and assertive way.

2. Be specific: When communicating your boundaries, be specific about what you will and will not tolerate. For example, if you do not want to be contacted outside of work hours, let others know exactly when you are available for work-related conversations.

3. Define emergencies: If you do not want to be contacted on vacation unless it is an emergency, make sure to clearly define what constitutes an emergency for you. This will help others understand when it is appropriate to reach out to you.

4. Address boundary violations immediately: If someone crosses your boundary, address it immediately. This sends a clear message that the behavior is not acceptable and will not be tolerated in the future.

5. Include a note in your email signature: This can help to set expectations for when others can reach you and also can help you to stick to your own boundaries.

6. Be consistent: It's important to be consistent in enforcing your boundaries. By being consistent, others will understand what is and is not acceptable behaviour.

7. Reflect and adapt: Review and reflect on your boundaries and needs on a regular basis, and make sure to adjust them as you learn more about yourself and the situation changes.

8. Practice: Communicating boundaries can be difficult at first, but with practice, it will become more natural and effective.

9. Set consequences: In some cases, setting consequences for boundary violations can be helpful. For example, if a coworker consistently contacts you outside of work hours, you may need to set a consequence such as not responding until the next work day.

10. Be mindful of cultural differences: Different cultures may have different ideas about boundaries, so it's important to be mindful of this and adjust your communication accordingly.

11. Use positive language: Instead of saying "I can't" or "I won't", use positive language such as "I prefer" or "I need". This can help to create a more positive and collaborative atmosphere.

12. Avoid blaming or attacking language: When communicating your boundaries, avoid using blaming or attacking language. Instead, focus on expressing your needs and feelings in a calm and respectful manner.

Setting and enforcing boundaries is essential to maintaining healthy relationships, both personally and professionally. By being clear about your needs and communicating them assertively, you can establish a mutual understanding and respect with others. Remember to reflect on and adapt your boundaries as needed, and to consistently enforce them to maintain healthy relationships. With practice, setting and enforcing boundaries will become a natural and effective part of your communication style.

Self-Assessment - Communicating Your Boundaries

Understanding and communicating personal boundaries is a critical aspect of maintaining a healthy and respectful work environment. This self-assessment provides an opportunity to reflect on your ability to express, negotiate, and maintain these boundaries effectively. By introspectively examining your skills, you'll be better prepared to improve your boundary-setting strategies and communication style at work.

For each question, please rate yourself on a scale of 1-5, where 1 represents "Strongly Disagree" and 5 represents "Strongly Agree."

1. I am comfortable using assertive communication techniques to express my boundaries at work.
2. I am prepared to face pushback when communicating my boundaries with others.
3. I can handle resistance and pushback effectively when setting boundaries.
4. I know my rights in the workplace and can assert them while maintaining my boundaries.
5. I am comfortable saying "no" at work when necessary to protect my boundaries.
6. I can say "no" at work politely and effectively without feeling guilty.
7. I use "I" messages when communicating my boundaries to ensure

clarity and avoid blame.

8.   I communicate my boundaries with confidence and clarity to others.

9.   I actively seek tips and strategies for effectively communicating my boundaries with co-workers and supervisors.

10.   I have experienced positive outcomes as a result of clearly communicating my boundaries.

11.   I can adapt my communication style to different situations while maintaining my boundaries.

12.   I know how to express my boundaries in a way that fosters mutual respect and understanding.

13.   I am able to maintain my boundaries even when faced with challenging or emotionally charged situations.

14.   I can recognize when my boundaries have been respected and express appreciation to others for acknowledging them.

15.   I am able to renegotiate my boundaries with others when necessary.

16.   I seek feedback from others to ensure my boundaries are clear and understood.

17.   I can maintain my boundaries while also being empathetic to the needs and concerns of others.

18.   I regularly reflect on my communication style and its impact on my boundary-setting.

19.   I have a support system in place to help me maintain my boundaries and deal with potential challenges.

20.   I am committed to continuously improving my communication skills to better protect and maintain my boundaries in the workplace.

Interpretation

Add up your total score and refer to the following scale:

80-100: Excellent boundary communication skills. Continue refining and strengthening your skills.

60-79: Good boundary communication skills. Identify areas for improvement and work on enhancing those aspects.

40-59: Moderate boundary communication skills. Focus on improving specific areas that need attention and practice.

20-39: Low boundary communication skills. Dedicate time and effort to learning and practicing effective communication techniques for setting boundaries.

0-19: Very low boundary communication skills. Consider seeking guidance from a professional or mentor to help improve your communication and boundary-setting abilities.

This assessment provides a comprehensive reflection on your ability to communicate and uphold your boundaries. Regularly revisiting and updating this assessment can be an effective tool for continuous growth and development. Remember, maintaining boundaries is an ongoing process, but by cultivating awareness and practicing assertive communication, you can ensure a respectful and balanced work environment.

Exercise: Communicating Your Boundaries

1. In your work environment, what are the aspects you feel most comfortable with, and which are those that often cause discomfort or stress? How could setting boundaries influence these areas?
2. How would you define your ideal work-life balance? What boundaries need to be in place to achieve this balance?
3. Can you identify a time when you established a boundary and received pushback? How did you handle it and what would you do differently next time?
4. If you anticipate resistance when setting a new boundary at work, how might you prepare for and address these concerns?
5. Reflect on a time you felt your rights were overlooked at work. How might you assert your rights in a similar situation in the future?
6. How well do you understand your rights in your workplace? Are

there areas you need to learn more about to ensure your boundaries are respected?

7. Recall an instance when you said 'yes' to a work request but wished you had said 'no'. What held you back and how might you handle it differently in the future?

8. How might you practice saying 'no' in low-stakes situations to build your confidence for more challenging scenarios?

9. Can you identify a recent work conflict where using 'I' messages could have led to a better outcome?

10. Reflect on your body language and tone during work interactions. How might these non-verbal cues impact the clarity and confidence of your communication?

11. Think of a boundary you would like to establish. What steps could you take to communicate this boundary confidently and effectively?

12. In what ways can you utilize active listening and empathy when communicating your boundaries, to create a more supportive and understanding work environment?

Chapter 7: Communicating Your Boundaries with Others

The most powerful communication tool you have is your own personal integrity." - Brian Tracy

The Journey Begins

As we navigate the complex tapestry of our professional lives, an essential skill often overlooked is the ability to define, articulate, and maintain our personal boundaries. The intricate dance of professional relationships—be it with colleagues, managers, or clients—requires a delicate balancing act. On one hand, we must meet the needs of the projects we undertake and respect the dynamics of our teams. On the other, we must preserve our personal integrity, the most powerful communication tool we possess.

A boundary, simply put, is the line that marks the limits of an area—the space between 'this is me' and 'this is not me.' It's the invisible frontier that defends our values, beliefs, mental and emotional health. In a professional context, boundaries serve as the pillars of our work ethic, the yardstick by which we measure what is acceptable to us in our interactions with others.

Communicating our boundaries effectively is akin to weaving a story. It's a tale that elucidates our needs, our limits, and, most importantly, our self-respect. It's a narrative that becomes an integral part of our professional persona, a testament to our personal integrity. This communication is not merely an act—it's a commitment to ourselves, a proclamation of our inherent worth, and a demonstration of our respect for others' boundaries in turn.

In the realm of collaborative projects, the articulation of boundaries becomes even more critical. Such environments are a fertile breeding ground for blurred lines and overstepped boundaries, as the convergence of multiple perspectives, ideas, and work styles often creates a delicate balance between individual responsibilities and group dynamics. Hence, it is in these situations that the ability to communicate your boundaries with clarity and conviction is paramount.

For instance, if you're tasked with a project that extends beyond your working hours, it's within your right—and indeed, your responsibility—to communicate your boundary. Express your commitment to the project while also highlighting the importance of maintaining a healthy work-life balance. It's in this direct, respectful communication that your personal integrity shines, acting as a compass that guides not just you but the whole team towards a more empathetic, respectful work environment.

Similarly, maintaining a professional relationship with clients involves a dance of boundaries. It's crucial to understand that while clients have their needs, you too have your limits and rights. Being able to express these boundaries helps cultivate a relationship that is based on mutual respect and understanding. It's about ensuring that in the quest to meet clients' needs, you don't end up compromising your values or well-being.

In essence, communicating your boundaries is an act of courage. It requires you to step into your power and make visible what is often invisible. It's about bringing to light the contours of your professional self, carving out a space that respects both your needs and those of others. It's about embodying your personal integrity, treating it not as an abstract concept but as a tangible, actionable tool for effective communication.

By recognizing that setting boundaries is not about building walls, but rather about nurturing healthy, respectful interactions. It's not about separating ourselves from others, but about defining who we are in relation to them. It's a continuous process, a journey of self-discovery, and a testament to our personal growth. And when done right, the act of setting and communicating boundaries can transform our professional relationships, fostering a culture of respect, empathy, and mutual understanding.

The Key to Team Prosperity

As organizations place greater emphasis on collaboration and teamwork to maintain their competitive edge and achieve success, it is essential for team members to understand their individual roles, responsibilities, and the manner in which they should interact with one another. This highlights the significance of setting clear boundaries within a team. When effectively established and communicated, boundaries provide the foundation for a strong, cohesive, and high-performing team.

When we lack clear boundaries, we often face challenges in communication, role clarification, and goal achievement. These challenges can be detrimental to our overall success. As such, it's crucial for us to recognize the importance of boundaries in our team dynamics, and strive to establish and maintain them from the outset. By doing so, we create a well-functioning, successful team that can navigate the complexities of the modern workplace with ease.

Establishing boundaries within a team is a critical element of team dynamics that facilitates the development of well-defined guidelines for behavior and communication. These boundaries are indispensable for fostering a structured and stable team environment, which ultimately cultivates a healthy and productive workplace. When team members are aware of the boundaries and expectations, they are less likely to indulge in actions that create friction or tension, and more inclined to collaborate efficiently and effectively.

In fact, boundaries serve to delineate clear roles and responsibilities for team members, enhancing accountability and minimizing confusion. Without such explicit boundaries, team members may engage in disruptive or detrimental behaviors, such as gossiping or avoiding responsibility for their work. This highlights the importance of instituting boundaries, which can foster trust and respect within the team, as team members know what to expect from one another and can depend on each other to fulfill their responsibilities.

Moreover, implementing boundaries within a team can mitigate conflicts and miscommunications. Team members who understand their roles and responsibilities, and operate within set boundaries, are less likely to engage in friction-causing behaviors. Transparent boundaries also encourage trust and respect within the team, as team members can anticipate each other's actions and depend on one another to fulfill their duties.

A key benefit of establishing boundaries in a team is the enhancement of overall performance and productivity. Team members are more apt to attain their goals and execute tasks efficiently when they comprehend their roles and responsibilities and cooperate within the set boundaries. This can result in heightened job satisfaction, as team members experience a sense of accomplishment and pride in their work. Additionally, it can help alleviate burnout, as team members possess a clear understanding of expectations and the support they can receive from others.

To illustrate this, consider the case of Owen, a member of a project team within his company. As the team begins working together, Owen realizes that there are some communication issues and confusion regarding roles and responsibilities. To address these concerns, Owen proposes that the team establishes clear boundaries for behavior and communication. He suggests defining specific roles and responsibilities for each member, establishing guidelines for communication, and identifying potential sources of conflict. By doing so, Owen believes that the team will be better equipped to collaborate effectively, minimize misunderstandings, and achieve their objectives.

Supported by his team, Owen leads the effort to establish these boundaries. They hold a meeting where they discuss and agree on specific roles and responsibilities, communication protocols, and ways to handle conflicts that may arise. By the end of the meeting, the team has a clear understanding of what is expected of them and how they should interact with one another.

In the following weeks, Owen and the team members continue to follow the established boundaries, and they begin to see improvements in their communication and productivity. With the reduced tension and clear guidelines for behavior and communication, they are able to focus on their work and accomplish their goals more efficiently. As a result, they feel more satisfied with their work, and Owen feels proud of the role he played in establishing the boundaries that helped make it possible.

Defining boundaries within a team is a vital component of team dynamics that paves the way for a thriving, productive, and efficient work atmosphere. By formulating distinct and specific parameters for behavior and communication, team members can effectively collaborate and achieve their objectives. Establishing boundaries helps to prevent conflicts, foster trust and respect, and elevate overall performance and productivity. This process should be ongoing, with regular assessments and adjustments as needed, to guarantee the team's enduring success.

A Toolbox for Setting Boundaries in Team Collaborations

Establishing healthy boundaries can prevent burnout, improve team dynamics, and ensure that everyone's needs are met. Here are 12 strategies for setting boundaries in a team project, emphasizing the importance of communication, assertiveness, and taking care of oneself.

1. Communicate your expectations and needs: Be clear about what you need in order to be successful on the project. This might include things like the amount of work you can handle, the amount of time you have available to work, or any specific resources you need.

2. Set limits on your availability: It's important to have time to rest and recharge, so make sure you're not always available to work on the project. Set boundaries around when you are and are not available to work.

3. Don't be afraid to say no: If you're asked to take on more work than you can handle, it's okay to say no. It's better to be honest about your limitations than to try to take on too much and risk burnout or poor quality work.

4. Be open to negotiation: Be open to negotiation and compromise. Sometimes, it may be necessary to adjust your boundaries or expectations in order to accommodate the needs of the team or project.

5. Prioritise self-care: Remember to take care of yourself and set aside time for self-care. It can be easy to get caught up in the demands of a team or group project, but taking care of yourself is important for maintaining your boundaries and avoiding burnout.

6. Have regular check-ins: Set a regular meeting for the team to check-in on the progress of the project and give everyone a chance to voice any concerns or issues they may have. This also helps to identify if any boundaries are not being respected and address them in a timely fashion.

7. Encourage open communication: Foster a constructive work atmosphere by encouraging open, honest communication among team members. This approach respects everyone's boundaries and cultivates a positive, respectful environment.

8. Establish clear roles and responsibilities: Make sure that everyone on the team knows their specific roles and responsibilities. This will help to reduce confusion and ensure that everyone is working on the tasks they are best suited for. This also helps to set clear expectations of what is expected from each team member.

9. Use technology tools: Utilise technology tools, such as project management software, to set and track deadlines and keep everyone on the team informed about the progress of the project. This can also be helpful for setting boundaries, as it allows team members to see when others are available to work and can help to coordinate schedules.

10. Create a positive team culture: Create a culture that emphasises respect and support for each other's boundaries. This can include things like regular team-building activities and encouraging team members to share their thoughts and ideas.

11. Address boundary-crossing behaviour promptly: If someone on the team is not respecting your boundaries, it's important to address it promptly. Speak with the person directly and let them know that their behaviour is not acceptable and how it is affecting you. This helps to establish and maintain a respectful working environment.

12. Take accountability: Lastly, take accountability for your actions and behaviour. Being aware of how you are interacting with your team, and taking steps to correct any negative patterns. It is important to lead by example and show that you respect your own boundaries and will advocate for them.

Remember, setting boundaries is not only about protecting yourself but also about respecting and understanding the needs of your fellow team members. By implementing these strategies you can effectively establish and maintain boundaries, promote open communication, and create a supportive team culture.

Defining Boundaries with Leadership

Navigating the professional relationship with your manager can be challenging, but setting boundaries is crucial for a healthy work-life balance. Here are 12 strategies to help you effectively communicate your expectations, maintain boundaries, and prioritize self-care, ultimately fostering a successful working relationship and a more fulfilling life.

1. Managerial Communication: Clearly communicate your expectations and needs to your manager. This includes your working hours, preferred communication methods, and any areas where you may need extra support or guidance.

2. Workload Boundaries: Establish clear boundaries around your workload and responsibilities. This may include delegating tasks to others or asking for help when you feel overwhelmed.

3. Power of Rejection: Learn to say no when necessary. It's important to be able to set boundaries around your time and energy and to be able to decline requests or tasks that are not within your scope of responsibility or that will not add value to your role.

4. Professional Communication: Communicate your needs and boundaries in a professional and respectful manner. It's important to remember that setting boundaries is not a sign of weakness, but rather a sign of strength and self-awareness.

5. Boundary Enforcement: Communicate your boundaries through actions as well. Follow up your words with actions. If you say you will only be working from 9-5, stick to that schedule. If you say you won't work on weekends, make sure you don't work on weekends.

6. Flexibility and Firmness: Be flexible with your boundaries but also be firm. Be open to negotiation but also be prepared to stick to your position if necessary.

7. Regular Reflection: Reflect on the situation and make adjustments when necessary. Regularly check in with yourself to assess whether your boundaries are working effectively, and make adjustments as necessary.

8. Documentation Importance: Keep a record of any instances where your boundaries were crossed. This can help you to better communicate your needs and concerns to your manager, and provide evidence if necessary.

9. Communication Strategy: Create a communication plan with your manager. Establish a regular schedule for touchpoints, such as weekly or monthly meetings, to discuss progress and address any issues that may arise.

10. Prioritize self-care: Setting boundaries with your manager can be emotionally and mentally taxing, so make sure to take time for yourself to relax, recharge and maintain a good work-life balance.

11. Practice assertiveness: Learn to speak up for yourself in a respectful and professional manner, and do not be afraid to defend your position when necessary.

12. Be open to feedback: Be open to hearing your manager's perspective, and be willing to make adjustments or changes as necessary to reach a mutually beneficial outcome.

By identifying your boundaries, communicating them clearly and respectfully, being open to feedback, and prioritizing self-care, you can build a strong foundation for a successful working relationship. Remember, advocating for your own well-being is not a sign of weakness, but rather a sign of strength, self-awareness, and professionalism.

Setting Boundaries with Clients

Achieving a balance between providing exceptional service and safeguarding our personal well-being is crucial in our professional lives. Working with clients can be an incredibly rewarding experience, yet it also presents its own set of challenges, particularly when it comes to setting boundaries. As professionals, recognizing our limitations and effectively communicating them to clients is essential, all while maintaining a high level of service and professionalism. By doing so, we can establish healthy, mutually beneficial relationships that foster long-term success.

Before engaging with clients, it's vital to gain a clear understanding of our values, priorities, and work ethic. This self-awareness serves as a foundation for setting boundaries and effectively communicating our expectations. Assessing our workload, the scope of the projects we take on, and the level of involvement we can realistically provide is crucial. This introspection allows us to identify our limitations and develop a plan to maintain a healthy work-life balance while still delivering exceptional results to our clients.

All too often, we may inadvertently allow clients to take advantage of us, driven by the fear of losing their business or causing dissatisfaction. This can lead to a detrimental, imbalanced dynamic where we find ourselves consistently exploited and overwhelmed with work. It is essential to recognize the importance of setting boundaries with clients to protect our own time, energy, and mental well-being.

Clients may develop unrealistic expectations, such as believing we should be accessible 24/7 or demanding a seemingly endless stream of revisions and last-minute alterations. Such expectations can place an immense burden on our shoulders, leading to stress, burnout, and reduced overall productivity. To counter these issues, we must take proactive measures by defining clear boundaries and effectively communicating our availability and limitations.

Establishing and maintaining boundaries can deter clients from attempting to manipulate or pressure us into tasks that we are uncomfortable with or that clash with our values and beliefs. This is crucial to preserving a sense of professionalism and mutual respect in the working relationship. By communicating our expectations and enforcing clear boundaries, we can position ourselves as leaders and professionals who are unwilling to compromise on their standards, integrity, and overall well-being.

Boundaries serve as essential tools for communication and provide a sense of security and stability for all parties involved. They clarify expectations, facilitate a balanced power dynamic, and prevent clients from exploiting our time and resources. Without boundaries, the client-professional relationship can easily devolve into a problematic and unhealthy situation.

One practical approach to setting boundaries is implementing office hours and explicitly informing clients of your unavailability outside those hours. This strategy helps create a clear distinction between personal and professional time, allowing for a better work-life balance. Additionally, being transparent about deadlines and holding clients accountable for meeting them can prevent last-minute requests and changes that induce stress and frustration.

It is essential to hone our emotional management skills, as guilt may arise when asserting ourselves and enforcing boundaries. We must remind ourselves that there is nothing wrong with protecting our interests and well-being. If a client attempts to manipulate or alter our boundaries, it could be an indication that the partnership is unsuitable. In such cases, it may be wiser to terminate the relationship rather than endure a toxic situation that could have lasting negative effects on our mental health and overall performance.

Consistently revisiting and re-evaluating our boundaries is also crucial. This practice allows us to identify any necessary adjustments and ensures that our boundaries remain relevant and effective. Open communication with clients about any changes to boundaries can foster understanding and prevent potential misunderstandings.

Brianna is a talented web developer who has been freelancing for a few years. She loves her job and enjoys working with clients to bring their visions to life. However, Brianna often finds herself struggling to set boundaries with her clients.

She has had clients who expect her to be accessible 24/7 and who demand last-minute changes or endless revisions. Brianna wants to provide excellent customer service, but she also recognizes that she needs to protect her time and energy.

After reading about the importance of setting boundaries, Brianna decides to make some changes to her approach. Firstly, she creates office hours and communicates them to her clients explicitly. She lets them know that she will be available during designated hours and will respond to their requests within a reasonable time frame.

Brianna also begins to set realistic deadlines and holds her clients accountable for meeting them. She knows that last-minute changes can be stressful and that it's essential to plan ahead to avoid any last-minute surprises.

Although Brianna feels guilty at times for saying no to a client or declining a project, she reminds herself that her well-being is essential. She knows that setting boundaries will help her work more efficiently, reduce stress and burnout, and improve her overall productivity.

By enforcing clear boundaries, Brianna positions herself as a professional who is unwilling to compromise on her standards and values. She maintains an open and honest line of communication with her clients, which helps to foster mutual respect and understanding.

In summary, establishing and maintaining boundaries with clients is vital for nurturing healthy and fruitful working relationships. By clearly communicating our expectations and limitations, safeguarding our own time and energy, and effectively managing our emotions, we can present ourselves as leaders and professionals who refuse to compromise on standards, integrity, and well-being. By doing so, we will be better equipped to forge more robust, mutually beneficial, and long-lasting partnerships with our clients, ultimately leading to a more fulfilling and successful professional journey.

Mastering Client Relations

Establishing healthy boundaries with clients is crucial for maintaining work-life balance and ensuring project success. By setting clear expectations, prioritizing well-being, and staying true to core values, you can effectively manage client relationships and deliver high-quality work. Here are 12 key strategies for creating and maintaining these boundaries.

1. **Embrace open and transparent communication:** This means being upfront about your expectations, availability, and capabilities. It also means being transparent about any potential challenges or obstacles that may arise during the course of the project.

2. **Define your time commitment:** Clearly communicate the time you can allocate to a client or project, establish suitable boundaries, and remain responsive to client needs.

3. **Set and adhere to boundaries:** Clearly delineate what you will and will not tolerate from clients, and remain steadfast in upholding these boundaries.

4. **Remain open to new opportunities:** This means being open to new opportunities and possibilities, and not getting too attached to any one project or client. It also means being willing to move on if a project or client is not working out.

5. **Uphold your core values:** Stay true to your values and beliefs, and refrain from compromising them for the sake of a client or project.

6. **Prioritize well-being over financial gain:** Remain mindful of your own well-being, and avoid sacrificing it for a client or project.

7. **Establish payment terms in advance:** Clearly outline your payment expectations and schedule, and remain responsive to client needs.

8. **Document everything in writing:** Maintain a written contract, agreement, and detailed records of all communications and transactions.

9. **Maintain control of the project:** Assert your authority by setting appropriate boundaries and expectations, while remaining responsive to client needs.

10. **Stand your ground:** If your client is out of control. Some clients

might not be aware they are crossing boundaries, so you need to let them know. This means being assertive and confident in your own abilities and worth, and not being afraid to stand up for yourself.

11. **Master the art of saying no:** Clients that take up too much of your time or bandwidth aren't worth it. This means being selective about the clients and projects you take on, and being willing to walk away from those that are not a good fit.

12. **Prioritize your well-being without guilt:** This means being true to yourself and your own needs and wants, and not compromising them for the sake of a client or project. It also means being willing to walk away from a project or client if necessary, and not feeling guilty or bad about it. It is important to remember that your well-being and happiness should always come first.

By adopting these strategies, you can foster an atmosphere of mutual respect, safeguard your well-being, and guarantee that your projects are completed on time and to the highest standard. Prioritizing your needs and staying true to your values will ultimately lead to better outcomes for both you and your clients. Remember that you possess the power to establish the rules and make decisions shaping your professional journey.

Self-Assessment - Communicating Your Boundaries with Others

The ability to effectively set and communicate personal boundaries is crucial for mental well-being and professional success. This self-assessment provides insight into how well you manage your boundaries in a variety of professional contexts, from team collaborations to client interactions. Use it as a tool to evaluate your capacity for boundary-setting, identify areas of strength, and recognize potential areas for growth.

Please rate each statement on a scale from 1 to 5, where 1 represents "Strongly Disagree" and 5 represents "Strongly Agree."

1. I am comfortable setting clear boundaries for team success and collaboration.
2. I effectively communicate my boundaries in team projects to

ensure my workload is manageable.

3. I have open and honest conversations with my co-workers about my boundaries and expectations.
4. I am able to set and maintain boundaries with clients and customers to protect my well-being.
5. I can easily identify triggers and stressors that may compromise my boundaries in the workplace.
6. I have developed healthy coping strategies for dealing with difficult colleagues and supervisors.
7. I effectively communicate my boundaries to others in various work situations, including team meetings and one-on-one conversations.
8. My professional relationships have improved as a result of effectively communicating my boundaries.
9. I maintain boundaries with others while fostering a positive work environment.
10. I am confident in my ability to navigate complex situations while maintaining my boundaries.
11. I can recognize when my boundaries are being tested or crossed in the workplace.
12. I communicate my needs assertively and respectfully when my boundaries are violated.
13. I am proactive in addressing potential boundary issues before they escalate.
14. I seek feedback from others to ensure my boundaries are clear and understood.
15. I am willing to adjust my boundaries when necessary to maintain a healthy work environment.
16. I collaborate with my team to establish shared boundaries that contribute to overall team success.
17. I have the ability to say "no" when necessary to protect my boundaries.
18. I am comfortable discussing my boundaries with clients and customers, even when it may be challenging.
19. I prioritize my own well-being and enforce my boundaries, even in high-pressure situations.

20. I continuously work on improving my boundary-setting skills and communication strategies.

To interpret the results of this self-assessment, add up the total score from all 20 questions. The maximum possible score is 100, and the minimum score is 20. Use the following scale to evaluate your overall boundary-setting and communication skills:

20-39: Needs Improvement

Your ability to set and communicate boundaries at work needs significant improvement. It's important to focus on developing your skills in asserting and maintaining boundaries, communicating effectively with others, and recognizing triggers and stressors. Consider seeking guidance from a mentor, reading books on boundary-setting, or attending workshops to help you build these skills.

40-59: Developing Skills

You have a basic understanding of boundary-setting and communication, but there is still room for growth. Continue to work on refining your skills in setting clear boundaries, communicating assertively, and managing complex situations. Seek feedback from colleagues and supervisors to identify specific areas for improvement.

60-79: Proficient

You have a good grasp of boundary-setting and communication in the workplace. You are able to set and maintain boundaries with co-workers, supervisors, and clients, and can effectively navigate most work situations. Continue to practice and strengthen your skills, and look for opportunities to support others in developing their own boundary-setting abilities.

80-100: Highly Skilled

Your boundary-setting and communication skills are exceptional. You are able to effectively establish and maintain boundaries in a variety of work situations and have developed strong coping strategies for dealing with challenging colleagues and supervisors. Continue to refine your skills and serve as a role model for others in the workplace.

As you reflect on your responses to this assessment, remember that establishing and maintaining boundaries is an ongoing process that requires continuous effort and self-awareness. The goal is not to achieve perfection, but to develop a balanced approach that contributes to healthier work relationships and a more productive work environment. By continuously refining your boundary-setting skills and communication strategies, you are taking proactive steps towards a more sustainable professional life.

Exercise: Communicating Your Boundaries with Others

1. Reflect on a situation where you felt overwhelmed with tasks assigned by your leader. What could you have done differently to communicate your capacity and set a boundary?
2. How do you currently communicate your need for personal time and space to your leaders? Is there room for improvement?
3. Have there been instances where you felt that your ideas or opinions were disregarded by leadership? How might you establish a boundary that fosters respect for your contributions?

1. Think about a challenging client relationship. What boundaries might you set to better manage your interactions?
2. How have you handled situations where a client has demanded more time or resources than agreed upon? How might setting clear boundaries upfront have changed the outcome?
3. How do you manage communications with clients outside of normal working hours? Is there a boundary that you can set to protect your personal time?

1. Are there any clients that you dread interacting with? What specific boundaries could you put in place to make these interactions less stressful?
2. How do you balance the needs of your clients with your own needs and the needs of your organization? Are there any boundaries that

could help create a healthier balance?

3. How have you handled situations when a client has crossed a professional boundary? What did you learn from these experiences and how can this guide future boundary-setting?

1. Can you recall an instance where a co-worker encroached on your personal or professional boundaries? What could you have done differently to uphold your boundaries?

2. How do you manage social interactions with co-workers in order to maintain a professional atmosphere? Are there clear boundaries in place?

3. Think about a time when you had to work closely with a co-worker with whom you had personal differences. How did you establish boundaries to ensure a productive work relationship?

Chapter 8: Setting Boundaries with Remote Work

"Setting boundaries is an act of honoring yourself and valuing your needs."

A Gateway to Balancing Remote Work

The rapid growth of remote work in recent years has been driven by advances in technology and an increasing emphasis on work-life balance. Although remote work offers numerous benefits such as flexibility, cost savings, and the ability to work from virtually anywhere, it also presents unique challenges that necessitate effective boundary-setting to maintain a healthy work-life balance.

Establishing boundaries in remote work is of paramount importance for several reasons. Firstly, maintaining a work-life balance is critical. Remote work often blurs the lines between work and personal life, making it essential for you to create clear distinctions between the two. This ensures increased satisfaction in both personal and professional realms and promotes improved mental health. Secondly, setting boundaries is crucial for reducing stress and burnout. If you do not establish boundaries, you run the risk of overworking, resulting in increased stress and burnout. By setting limits on work hours and responsibilities, you can avoid the negative impacts of stress and maintain overall well-being. Lastly, proper boundary-setting enhances productivity and focus. By creating a dedicated workspace and adhering to a consistent schedule, you can maintain a high level of efficiency and contribute effectively to your team.

Despite the many advantages of remote work, it also poses several unique challenges that can make it difficult to establish and maintain healthy boundaries. One such challenge is the increased flexibility and blurred lines between work and personal life. While this flexibility enables you to tailor your schedule to accommodate personal needs, it can also make it challenging to disconnect from work, leading to an imbalance between work and personal life. Another challenge faced by you when working remotely is the difficulty in separating work and home environments. Working from home often means that you share your work environment with your personal space, making it difficult to create a clear distinction between the two. This can potentially lead to distractions, decreased productivity, and difficulty establishing a professional atmosphere. Lastly, navigating communication and expectations with co-workers and supervisors can be challenging in remote work. Remote work relies heavily on digital communication, which can present difficulties in terms of establishing rapport, building relationships, and ensuring clear communication. Additionally, setting expectations and boundaries with co-workers and supervisors can be difficult when working remotely, as there may be a lack of face-to-face interaction and varying levels of understanding regarding remote work dynamics.

In the subsequent sections, we will delve into strategies and best practices for setting effective boundaries in remote work. By addressing the unique challenges mentioned above, we aim to ensure a healthy work-life balance for you as a remote worker.

Balancing the Scale

The prevalence of remote work has increased significantly in recent years, offering us the convenience and flexibility that comes with working from home. However, this arrangement can make it challenging to maintain a healthy work-life balance. The absence of clear boundaries between work and personal time can lead to excessive working hours and the neglect of our personal life. To effectively manage these challenges, we must establish personal boundaries and adhere to guidelines that differentiate work time from personal time.

One of the primary challenges we face as remote workers is the blurred line between our work and personal lives. While working in an office setting naturally separates work from personal life, it becomes more challenging to disengage from work when at home. This often leads to burnout, decreased motivation, and a negative impact on our overall well-being. To counteract this, it is crucial to define personal boundaries that align with our priorities and values.

Establishing personal boundaries begins with understanding our unique priorities and values, then setting boundaries that support these goals. For instance, if we prioritize spending time with our family, we should consider setting a boundary that prevents work from spilling into our evenings, allowing for quality time with loved ones. Similarly, if we value our physical and mental health, we should set a boundary that includes taking regular breaks throughout the day to stretch, move around, or engage in activities that help us recharge.

After defining our personal boundaries, we should create both physical and mental boundaries to reinforce them. To establish physical boundaries, we can designate a specific workspace in our home separate from personal spaces. This separation helps create a distinction between work and personal time, making it easier to disengage from work when necessary. Establishing mental boundaries could involve setting a designated time to end work each day and committing not to check work emails or take work calls outside of working hours.

Effectively communicating our boundaries is essential when working remotely. This involves clearly conveying our boundaries to colleagues, managers, and family members. Direct communication and assertiveness may be required to ensure our boundaries are respected. For remote workers, informing colleagues of our availability and personal time can help prevent misunderstandings and ensure everyone is on the same page.

Additionally, setting boundaries with those we live with is crucial for maintaining a productive work environment. We should establish a designated work area in our home, free from distractions, and communicate to our family or roommates that interruptions should be limited to emergencies during work hours. Set specific times for breaks and lunch, when we can engage in socializing or other non-work activities. Regular check-ins can help address any concerns and ensure everyone understands and respects our work schedule.

Finally, we should maintain accountability and flexibility by periodically evaluating our adherence to our boundaries and making necessary adjustments. Stay open-minded and willing to adapt our boundaries if our current approach is not effective. For example, if we find ourselves working longer hours than desired, we should re-evaluate our boundaries to ensure we are taking the necessary personal time. Establishing a healthy work-life balance as a remote worker may be challenging, but it is possible with the right approach.

Phoenix is a software developer who recently started working from home. He loves the flexibility and convenience of being able to work from his own space, but he's finding it hard to switch off from work at the end of the day. He often finds himself working longer hours and neglecting his personal life. Phoenix realizes that he needs to set clear boundaries to maintain a healthy work-life balance.

To start, Phoenix identifies his personal priorities and values, and sets boundaries that align with those goals. He values spending time with his family, so he decides to set a boundary that he will not work after 6 pm in the evening so that he can have dinner and spend time with his loved ones. He also values his physical and mental health, so he sets a boundary that he will take a break every hour to move around and stretch.

To create physical boundaries, Phoenix sets up a dedicated workspace in his home that is separate from his personal spaces. This helps him create a clear distinction between work and personal time and makes it easier for him to switch off when he is not working. To create mental boundaries, Phoenix sets a specific time each day when he will stop working and commits to not checking his work email or taking work calls outside of that time.

Phoenix communicates his boundaries to his colleagues, managers, and family members. He lets his colleagues know when he will be available to work and when he will be taking time for himself, to prevent confusion and ensure that everyone is on the same page. He also establishes a designated work area in his home that is free from distractions and communicates his schedule clearly to his family, asking that they respect his working hours.

Phoenix checks in with himself regularly to ensure that he is adhering to his boundaries and makes any necessary adjustments. He stays accountable and flexible and adapts his boundaries as needed. Phoenix realizes that with the right approach, it is possible to set effective work-life boundaries while working from home, and he can enjoy the many benefits of working remotely.

Remote work offers numerous benefits, but maintaining a healthy work-life balance requires deliberate effort. By identifying personal boundaries, creating physical and mental boundaries, effectively communicating our boundaries to others, and maintaining accountability and flexibility, we can strike the right balance between our work and personal life, ultimately reaping the rewards of working from home.

Creating a Designated Workspace

Many of us struggle with creating a designated workspace at home for various reasons. One common reason is a lack of space or resources. With limited square footage, it can be difficult for us to find an area that can be solely dedicated to work. Some of us may also lack the financial means to invest in the necessary equipment or furnishings to create an effective workspace. Moreover, for those living with others, it may be challenging to negotiate shared spaces or find an area that provides the required privacy and quiet.

Another reason we may not create a designated workspace is a lack of understanding of its importance. With the increasing prevalence of remote work, some of us may not have experienced the benefits of a dedicated workspace or may underestimate the impact it can have on productivity and work-life balance. We may assume that working from any area in our home, such as the kitchen table or couch, is sufficient for our needs. However, this approach often leads to blurred boundaries between work and personal life, making it difficult for us to maintain focus and fully disengage from work-related tasks during personal time.

Furthermore, we may be resistant to change, particularly if we have developed habits or routines that do not involve a designated workspace.

Some of us may find it challenging to break away from our established patterns, fearing that change might disrupt our productivity or comfort. However, creating a designated workspace is a crucial step in fostering a healthy work-life balance and improving overall well-being. By overcoming these obstacles, we can experience the numerous advantages of having a dedicated space for work, including enhanced focus, increased productivity, and a more professional atmosphere.

Establishing a designated workspace is a crucial aspect of setting boundaries in remote work. Creating a dedicated area for your professional tasks allows you to separate your work and personal life more effectively, leading to increased productivity and focus. A dedicated workspace offers several benefits, such as improved concentration, clear work-life separation, and a professional atmosphere. Having a separate space for work minimizes distractions and allows you to concentrate more fully on your tasks, enhancing your efficiency and effectiveness. Additionally, a designated workspace serves as a visual cue, signalling when it's time to work and when it's time to engage in personal activities. This separation helps maintain a healthy work-life balance and reduces the risk of burnout. Furthermore, a dedicated workspace ensures that you have a suitable environment for video calls, meetings, and other professional interactions, creating a more professional image for you and your company.

To create an effective home office, it is essential to choose a location with minimal distractions, invest in ergonomic furniture, ensure proper lighting, organize your workspace, and personalize your space. Selecting a quiet area of your home, away from high-traffic zones and noisy activities, will help you stay focused and minimize interruptions during your work hours. Your comfort and well-being are crucial for productivity, so investing in an ergonomic chair, desk, and other necessary furniture will promote good posture and minimize the risk of strain or injury. Making sure your workspace has sufficient natural and artificial lighting will reduce eye strain and create a comfortable working environment. Keeping your workspace clutter-free and organized fosters a sense of control and efficiency. Lastly, adding personal touches to your workspace, such as photos, artwork, or motivational quotes, will create a comfortable and inspiring environment.

If you live with family members, roommates, or a partner, it's crucial to establish boundaries within your shared living space. Some strategies for setting boundaries in shared living situations include communicating your needs, creating physical boundaries, setting clear rules and expectations, and being flexible and adaptable. Initiating a conversation with those you live with regarding your work schedule, your need for a quiet and focused environment, and any specific requirements you may have can help set expectations and prevent misunderstandings. If possible, designate a separate room or partitioned area as your workspace and use physical barriers, such as room dividers or curtains, to separate your workspace from shared living areas. Establish rules concerning noise levels, interruptions, and shared responsibilities during your work hours, making sure that everyone in the household is aware of and agrees to these rules to minimize conflicts and distractions. Coexisting with others may sometimes require you to adapt your work schedule or environment to accommodate their needs, so be open to compromise and find inventive solutions to balance everyone's requirements.

By creating a designated workspace and establishing boundaries within a shared living space, you can more effectively separate your work and personal life. This separation will improve your overall productivity and work-life balance as a remote worker.

Defining Work Hours and Schedule

One of the most critical aspects of setting boundaries in remote work is defining your work hours and schedule. Establishing a regular work schedule creates a sense of structure, which is essential for productivity and maintaining a healthy work-life balance. A consistent schedule allows you to allocate time effectively for tasks and priorities, enabling you to accomplish more within your work hours. By clearly defining your work hours, you create a boundary between your professional and personal life, ensuring that one does not intrude upon the other. A structured work schedule also helps prevent overworking and enables you to allocate time for relaxation and self-care, reducing stress and the risk of burnout. Furthermore, a regular work schedule communicates to your co-workers and supervisors that you are committed to your work and available during specific hours, fostering a sense of accountability and professionalism.

Effective time and task management is crucial for maintaining productivity and achieving a balanced work-life dynamic in remote work. Consider strategies such as prioritizing tasks, using time-blocking techniques, setting realistic deadlines, taking regular breaks, and utilizing productivity tools to manage your time and tasks efficiently. Begin your day by identifying your most important tasks and focusing on completing them first. Allocate specific blocks of time for different tasks or categories of work, such as meetings, deep work, and administrative tasks. Establish achievable deadlines for your tasks and communicate them to your team to promote accountability and ensure that you and your team are on the same page regarding expectations. Incorporate short breaks throughout your workday to recharge and maintain focus. Utilize digital tools and apps for task management, time tracking, and collaboration to stay organized and efficient in your work.

While remote work offers the advantage of flexibility, it is essential to strike a balance between flexibility and structure to maintain productivity and a healthy work-life balance. Establish specific core working hours during which you will be available for meetings, collaboration, and communication with your team. Keep your co-workers and supervisors informed about your working hours and any changes in your schedule. Clear communication helps manage expectations and promotes a collaborative work environment. Communicate your work hours and expectations to your family and friends, asking them to respect your work time and minimize distractions. Lastly, be mindful of your personal needs and take advantage of the flexibility remote work offers to accommodate personal needs, such as exercise, family time, and self-care.

By defining your work hours and schedule, employing effective time and task management strategies, and balancing flexibility and structure, you can set clear boundaries in your remote work environment. This approach promotes productivity, a healthy work-life balance, and overall well-being as a remote worker.

Communicating Boundaries to Co-workers and Managers

Effectively communicating your boundaries to co-workers and supervisors is crucial for maintaining a healthy remote work environment. Being transparent about your availability and work hours helps manage expectations and ensures that everyone is on the same page. Share your work schedule with your team on a shared calendar, include your working hours and contact information in your email signature, and utilize the status feature on collaboration tools to indicate your current availability. These measures allow your colleagues to view your schedule and plan meetings or collaboration times accordingly.

Maintaining open communication with your remote colleagues is essential for effective collaboration and fostering a positive work environment. Schedule regular check-ins with your team members, either individually or as a group, to discuss ongoing projects, address concerns, and provide updates. Embrace video calls for discussions that require in-depth conversation, brainstorming sessions, or when providing feedback. Foster a culture of open feedback within your team, where colleagues feel comfortable sharing their thoughts, concerns, and ideas. Actively solicit input during meetings or create dedicated channels for feedback on collaboration tools.

It is essential to not only communicate your boundaries but also respect the boundaries of your co-workers and supervisors. Managing expectations and understanding others' limits contribute to a supportive and productive remote work environment. Be mindful of time zones when scheduling meetings or setting deadlines, and provide ample time for remote colleagues to complete tasks. If you are unsure about a colleague's availability or expectations, do not hesitate to ask for clarification. This helps prevent miscommunication and ensures that everyone is on the same page. Recognize that your co-workers have personal lives outside of work and avoid sending work-related messages or requesting tasks during their non-working hours, unless it is an urgent matter.

For example, if your co-worker has clearly communicated that they are unavailable after 6 pm, refrain from sending them work-related messages after that time. Instead, wait until the next working day or schedule a meeting within their designated work hours to discuss the matter.

By effectively communicating your boundaries to co-workers and supervisors, maintaining open communication with remote colleagues, and managing expectations while respecting others' boundaries, you can create a more harmonious and productive remote work environment. This, in turn, contributes to a healthier work-life balance and overall well-being as a remote worker.

Managing Distractions and Interruptions

Working remotely comes with its own unique set of distractions and interruptions that can hinder productivity and focus. Some common distractions in a remote work environment include constantly checking social media, email notifications, tackling household chores during work hours, sharing your living space with family members, roommates, or pets, and dealing with noise and external disruptions. To effectively manage these challenges, it's essential to first identify the distractions that are most relevant to your situation.

Once you've identified the common distractions in your remote work environment, it's essential to develop strategies to minimize interruptions and stay focused. Creating a designated workspace can help you separate your work and personal life, reducing distractions and improving focus. Allocate specific time blocks for deep work, during which you can minimize distractions by turning off digital notifications and setting your communication tools to "Do Not Disturb" mode. For example, you might schedule a two-hour block of uninterrupted work time every morning to tackle your most critical tasks. If noise is a significant distraction, consider investing in noise-cancelling headphones or using white noise apps to create a more focused work environment. Establish routines and breaks to help you transition into work mode and maintain focus throughout the day.

In a remote work setting, it's crucial to set clear boundaries with family and friends to minimize distractions and interruptions during your work hours. Inform your family members, roommates, or friends about your work hours and ask them to respect your time by minimizing interruptions and noise levels during those hours. For instance, you might let your family know that you are unavailable for non-emergency matters between 9 am and 12 pm. Use visual cues, such as a closed door, a "Do Not Disturb" sign, or wearing headphones, to signal that you are working and should not be interrupted. Share your work schedule with your family members or roommates using a shared calendar, highlighting important meetings or deadlines, so they are aware of your commitments. Develop agreements with your family members or roommates regarding household responsibilities and noise levels during work hours, ensuring that everyone is respectful of each other's work requirements. For example, you might agree to take turns handling household chores, such as laundry or dishwashing, so that they don't interfere with your work.

By identifying common distractions, implementing strategies to minimize interruptions, and setting boundaries with family and friends, you can create a more focused and productive remote work environment. This will not only improve your efficiency and output but also contribute to a healthier work-life balance in the long run.

Prioritizing Self-Care and Mental Health

While remote work offers numerous benefits, such as flexibility and the comfort of working from home, it can also impact mental health. The lack of face-to-face interaction with co-workers, blurred lines between work and personal life, and potential feelings of isolation can contribute to increased stress, anxiety, and burnout. Therefore, it is essential to prioritize self-care and mental well-being to maintain a healthy work-life balance.

Creating a daily routine that supports well-being is crucial for maintaining mental health while working remotely. Begin your day with activities that set a positive tone, such as meditation, exercise, or journaling. For example, starting your day with a 20-minute yoga session followed by a nutritious breakfast can help prepare you for a productive day. Establish and stick to consistent work hours to separate your work and personal life, reducing the risk of overworking and burnout. Include regular physical activity in your daily routine, as exercise can help alleviate stress and improve your mood. You could take a walk during lunchtime or participate in an online workout class after work. Furthermore, make an effort to plan and prepare balanced meals and snacks that fuel your body throughout the day, as eating well is essential for maintaining energy levels and overall well-being.

In addition to establishing a daily routine, taking breaks and incorporating relaxation into your workday is essential for maintaining mental health and reducing stress. Plan short breaks throughout your workday, allowing yourself time to recharge and refocus. For example, schedule a 5-minute break every hour to stretch or grab a glass of water. Utilize mindfulness techniques, such as deep breathing or meditation, during your breaks to help relieve stress and maintain mental clarity. A simple 5-minute breathing exercise can help you regain focus and calm your mind. Spend your breaks doing activities that bring you joy and relaxation, such as reading, listening to music, or engaging in a hobby. For instance, you might spend a 15-minute break tending to your indoor plants or playing with your pet. Physically distance yourself from your workspace during breaks to mentally disconnect from work. This could mean taking a walk outside, enjoying a cup of tea in another room, or simply sitting in a different area of your home.

By prioritizing self-care and mental health, establishing a daily routine that supports well-being, and incorporating breaks and relaxation into your workday, you can maintain a healthy work-life balance while working remotely. Taking care of yourself will not only benefit your mental well-being but also contribute to your overall productivity and job satisfaction.

Utilizing Technology to Enforce Boundaries

Technology can play a significant role in enforcing boundaries while working remotely. By embracing various tools and apps, you can effectively manage your time and boost productivity. Time tracking tools like Toggl and RescueTime can help you track the time spent on tasks, allowing you to identify inefficiencies and better manage your work hours. For instance, using RescueTime, you can discover how much time you spend on social media versus essential tasks and adjust your habits accordingly. Task management apps like Trello, Asana, or Todoist can help you organize and prioritize your work, ensuring you stay focused on your most important tasks. By creating a Trello board for your projects, you can have a visual representation of your workload and progress. Implementing time management techniques, such as the Pomodoro Technique, encourages you to work in short, focused intervals with breaks in between. Tools like TomatoTimer or Focus@Will can help you maintain focus throughout the day using this method.

Effective communication is crucial for setting boundaries with co-workers and supervisors in a remote work environment. Utilizing communication tools strategically can help establish and maintain your boundaries. Use messaging platforms like Slack or Microsoft Teams to convey your availability, work hours, and preferences. For example, you can set a custom status on Slack to indicate when you are busy or unavailable. Schedule meetings via video conferencing platforms like Zoom or Google Meet to foster connection and collaboration while maintaining your boundaries. You can set "office hours" for virtual meetings to ensure they don't interfere with your focused work time. Be strategic with your email communication by setting expectations around response times and utilizing features like "snooze" or "send later" to manage your inbox effectively.

Managing digital clutter and notifications is essential for maintaining focus and enforcing boundaries. To minimize distractions caused by digital clutter, consider disabling notifications for social media, news, and other non-work-related apps during work hours. Adjust the settings of your communication tools, such as Slack or email, to only receive notifications for essential updates or messages. For example, you can choose to be notified only when you are directly mentioned in a conversation. Additionally, keeping your computer desktop and folders organized and closing any unnecessary tabs or applications during work hours can minimize distractions and help you maintain focus.

By utilizing technology effectively, you can enforce boundaries, manage your time efficiently, and maintain focus while working remotely. Embracing these tools and strategies will help you create a more productive and balanced remote work experience.

Adjusting Boundaries as Needed

Establishing boundaries is an ongoing process that requires regular evaluation and adjustment. It's essential to recognize when your current boundaries may no longer be serving you well. Some signs that it's time to re-evaluate your boundaries include persistent stress or burnout, changes in personal or professional priorities, and feedback from co-workers or supervisors. If you continually feel overwhelmed, stressed, or burned out, despite having set boundaries, it may be time to reassess and make necessary adjustments.

As your work circumstances or personal life change, you may need to adjust your boundaries to maintain a healthy balance. For instance, if your team begins to work more closely with colleagues in different time zones, you may need to adjust your work hours to ensure effective collaboration while still preserving your work-life balance. Similarly, if you move to a new home or experience changes in your living situation, you may need to reassess your workspace and create new boundaries to maintain a productive work environment. Family changes, such as having a new baby or caring for an elderly family member, may also require you to create new boundaries, setting specific hours for caregiving responsibilities while still fulfilling your work commitments.

Continual self-reflection is vital for personal and professional growth in a remote work environment. By regularly evaluating your boundaries, you can ensure they align with your current needs and priorities. Schedule regular check-ins with yourself to assess your work-life balance, productivity, and overall well-being. Use this time to identify areas where your boundaries may need adjustment. Request feedback from co-workers, supervisors, and family members to gain insights into how well your boundaries are working and identify areas for improvement. Embrace a growth mindset, viewing your boundaries as flexible and adaptable, rather than fixed. This mindset will enable you to grow and adjust your boundaries as your work circumstances and personal life evolve.

By recognizing when to re-evaluate your boundaries, adapting to changes in your work circumstances and personal life, and engaging in ongoing self-reflection and growth, you can maintain a healthy work-life balance in remote work. Continuously adjusting your boundaries ensures that they remain relevant and effective, promoting a more satisfying and productive remote work experience.

The Future of Boundary Setting in Remote Work

In conclusion, setting healthy boundaries in remote work is crucial for long-term success and well-being. Establishing and maintaining effective boundaries can lead to numerous benefits, including improved work-life balance, increased productivity, enhanced mental health, and strengthened relationships with co-workers, supervisors, and family members. Boundaries enable you to separate work from personal life, preventing burnout and allowing you to enjoy your time outside of work more fully. By setting clear expectations and managing your time efficiently, you can stay focused on your most important tasks and achieve better results with your work.

As you continue your remote work journey, it's essential to embrace balance and prioritize personal growth in your career. By focusing on self-care, open communication, and adaptability, you can cultivate a remote work experience that supports your well-being and professional development. Regularly prioritize your mental and physical health by incorporating activities such as exercise, meditation, and hobbies into your daily routine. Maintain open lines of communication with co-workers and supervisors, sharing your needs, expectations, and any challenges you face.

Stay adaptable and remain open to change, willing to reassess your boundaries as your work circumstances and personal life evolve. By setting and maintaining healthy boundaries in your remote work, you can enjoy long-term benefits that contribute to a successful and fulfilling career. Embracing balance and personal growth will help you navigate the unique challenges of remote work and create a more satisfying and productive work experience.

Looking ahead to the future, advancements in technology and shifts in societal norms will likely continue to impact how we set boundaries in remote work. The proliferation of AI-powered productivity tools, digital wellness applications, and virtual reality interfaces will provide new ways to structure our work, manage our time, and separate our personal lives from our professional responsibilities. For instance, AI could be used to automate routine tasks, freeing up more time for creative and strategic work. Virtual reality could create immersive work environments that are distinct from our personal spaces, providing a clearer separation between work and home. In this way, future technologies could help to enforce and respect boundaries, enabling remote workers to achieve a better work-life balance and a higher level of productivity.

However, these advancements also pose new challenges. As technology continues to blur the line between our work and personal lives, it will become increasingly important to establish firm boundaries and resist the temptation to be "always on." Remote workers may need to take extra measures to protect their personal time and mental health, such as setting strict working hours, taking regular breaks, and turning off work-related notifications outside of these hours.

As we navigate the future of boundary setting in remote work, it will be essential to balance the benefits of new technologies with the need for personal space and downtime.

Self-Assessment - Setting Boundaries with Remote Work

As the world continues to adapt to the new normal of remote work, setting and maintaining boundaries becomes essential to ensure productivity, well-being, and work-life balance. This self-assessment is designed to help you evaluate your current practices, identify areas of improvement, and guide you in establishing effective boundaries within your remote work setup.

For each question, rate yourself on a scale of 1 to 5, where 1 = Never, 2 = Rarely, 3 = Sometimes, 4 = Often, and 5 = Always.

1. Do you have a designated workspace in your home for remote work?
2. Do you set clear and consistent work hours for yourself when working remotely?
3. Do you communicate your work schedule and availability to your co-workers and supervisors?
4. Are you able to maintain focus and productivity during your designated work hours?
5. Do you take regular breaks throughout the day to avoid burnout and maintain a healthy work-life balance?
6. Are you able to effectively manage distractions and interruptions during your work hours?
7. Do you utilize tools and technology to enforce your work boundaries (e.g., setting "Do Not Disturb" on messaging apps, using calendar blocks)?
8. Do you prioritize self-care and mental health while working remotely (e.g., exercise, mindfulness, hobbies)?
9. Are you able to disconnect from work-related tasks and technology during your non-work hours?
10. Do you maintain open communication with co-workers and supervisors about your remote work boundaries and expectations?
11. Are you able to delegate tasks and collaborate effectively with your team while working remotely?
12. Do you regularly assess your remote work boundaries and make adjustments as needed?
13. Do you feel comfortable discussing any challenges or concerns

related to remote work with your supervisor?

14. Do you set realistic goals and expectations for yourself when working remotely?

15. Do you maintain a healthy balance between work and personal life while working remotely?

16. Are you able to effectively manage your workload and prioritize tasks in a remote work setting?

17. Do you have a routine or rituals that help you transition between work and personal time?

18. Do you feel supported by your organization in maintaining your remote work boundaries?

19. Have you developed strategies for coping with feelings of isolation or disconnection while working remotely?

20. Do you feel confident in your ability to maintain resilience and adapt to changes in your remote work environment?

Interpretation

Add up your total score and refer to the following scale:

20-39: Limited Boundaries

Your remote work boundaries are limited, and you may struggle to maintain a healthy work-life balance. Consider re-evaluating your current approach and implementing new strategies to create a more sustainable remote work experience.

40-59: Developing Boundaries

You have started to establish some remote work boundaries, but there is still room for improvement. Reflect on the areas where you scored lower and consider implementing changes to strengthen your boundaries and enhance your work-life balance.

60-79: Balanced Boundaries

You have a good balance of remote work boundaries in place, allowing you to maintain a healthy work-life balance most of the time. Continue to monitor your boundaries and make adjustments as needed to maintain this balance.

80-99: Strong Boundaries

You have strong remote work boundaries in place, and you are likely experiencing a healthy work-life balance. Keep up the good work and continue to monitor your boundaries to ensure they remain effective.

100-120: Exceptional Boundaries

You have exceptional remote work boundaries in place, and your work-life balance is likely well-maintained. Continue to monitor your boundaries, and consider sharing your strategies with others who may benefit from your approach.

Through this assessment, you have explored various aspects of your remote work, from the physical workspace and time management to mental health and communication. The insights you've gained will empower you to refine your strategies and create a more balanced, fulfilling, and productive work experience. Remember, boundaries are crucial for your overall well-being and it's essential to continuously reassess and adapt them according to your evolving needs and circumstances.

Exercise: Setting Boundaries with Remote Work

1. Reflect on your current work-life balance. Are you satisfied with it? If not, what specific actions can you take to achieve a better balance between your work and personal life when working remotely?
2. How does your current workspace contribute to or detract from your productivity and focus? What modifications can you make to improve it, and how can you ensure it remains a space solely for work?
3. Do you find yourself consistently working outside your set work hours? What steps can you take to ensure you stick to your defined schedule and avoid overworking?

4. How comfortable do you feel communicating your work boundaries to your co-workers and managers? What steps can you take to improve this communication if it feels challenging?

5. Identify the three most frequent distractions or interruptions you face during your workday. How can you manage these proactively to improve your productivity?

6. How often do you integrate self-care practices into your daily routine? What new routines can you establish to better prioritize your mental health?

7. How are you currently utilizing technology to enforce your work boundaries? Are there other tools or strategies you could use to improve in this area?

8. When was the last time you reassessed and adjusted your work boundaries? How can you ensure that you are regularly checking in with yourself and making necessary adjustments?

9. On a scale of 1-10, how would you rate your current ability to set and maintain healthy work boundaries? What specific areas do you need to focus on to improve this score?

10. How have your work boundaries affected your relationships with your co-workers, managers, and people in your personal life? What changes, if any, would you like to make?

11. Can you recall a recent instance where your work boundaries were violated? How did you handle the situation, and what could you do differently in the future?

12. How effective are your current boundaries in contributing to a healthier work and personal life? What changes do you need to make to ensure these boundaries are more effective?

Chapter 9: Managing Boundary Violations

"Strength and growth come only through continuous effort and struggle." -
Napoleon Hill

Bridging the Gap

Boundaries, like the walls of a fortress, define and protect our personal and professional identities. The challenge, however, lies not in the mere establishment of these boundaries, but in their ongoing management and reinforcement. This chapter delves into the complexities of boundary management, providing valuable insights for navigating potential boundary violations with confidence.

Managing boundaries is often likened to an arduous journey. As the saying goes, "strength and growth come only through continuous effort and struggle." This struggle is integral to boundary management. It is in the continuous effort to assert our personal and professional boundaries that we grow and strengthen our understanding of our own worth and identity.

Yet, this journey is anything but straightforward. The complexities surrounding boundary management are as intricate as the human experience itself. Interpersonal dynamics, cultural expectations, personal vulnerabilities – they all contribute to a delicate tapestry where boundaries are ceaselessly negotiated.

Boundary violations, unfortunately, are not uncommon. They may range from minor encroachments to more severe invasions, each carrying the potential to upset our sense of self and security. It is essential, therefore, to recognize these violations, understand their triggers, and develop effective strategies to address them.

But how do we recognize these violations? It begins with mindfulness. Being mindful of our interactions with others enables us to perceive subtle signs of disrespect or overstepping. This heightened awareness, combined with a deep understanding of our own boundaries, empowers us to respond proactively rather than reactively to potential violations.

Addressing boundary violations requires fortitude and assertiveness. It's about reinforcing our boundaries in a manner that makes them an integral part of our personal and professional identity. It's about asserting our rights and our needs, not as an afterthought, but as a foundational principle of our interactions.

Yet, as much as we may aspire for perfect boundary management, we must acknowledge the emotional challenges that may arise when setting boundaries. Fear of conflict, fear of rejection, guilt – these are all potent emotions that can dissuade us from asserting our boundaries. It is essential to recognize these feelings, validate them, and yet not let them deter us from our path. It is a delicate balance, one that requires emotional intelligence and resilience. It is important to understand that boundaries are not set in stone. They evolve as we grow, reflecting our changing needs, expectations, and life circumstances. This fluidity is not a sign of weakness, but a testament to our ability to adapt and grow. It is this adaptive quality of boundaries that enables us to navigate the complexities of our lives with confidence and grace.

Boundary management is a continuous journey of struggle, growth, and empowerment. It requires mindfulness, assertiveness, emotional resilience, and adaptability. As we navigate the complex web of interpersonal relationships, our boundaries serve as both our shield and our guide, enabling us to protect and assert our personal and professional identity with confidence. They are the silent markers of our growth, the invisible threads that weave together the tapestry of our lives. So let us celebrate our boundaries, for they are the signposts on our journey towards personal growth and self-empowerment.

The Red Flags

A harmonious and productive work environment is built on mutual respect and understanding of personal and professional boundaries. However, boundary violations can often occur, disrupting the balance within a workplace and causing stress, burnout, and strained relationships. In order to maintain a healthy work environment, it is crucial for you to identify and address these boundary violations.

One type of boundary violation that can disrupt the workplace is time and workload violations. These occur when you are expected to work beyond your agreed-upon hours or take on tasks that are beyond your capacity. This can result from poor management, unrealistic expectations, or inadequate communication. Over time, these violations can lead to burnout, decreased job satisfaction, and reduced productivity. To compound this issue, emotional labor is another important aspect of boundary violations.

Emotional labor refers to the process of managing emotions in the workplace, often to meet job requirements or maintain a professional demeanor. When you are expected to constantly suppress your emotions or take on the emotional burdens of others without proper support, this can be considered a boundary violation. This emotional toll can lead to mental health issues and negatively impact your well-being. Furthermore, privacy and personal space are also essential components of healthy workplace boundaries.

In this category, boundary violations include looking through your personal items or information, making inappropriate physical contact, or invading your workspace. These violations can make you feel uncomfortable and create a hostile work environment. In addition, authority and decision-making boundaries ensure that everyone's roles and responsibilities are clearly defined in a workplace setting. Violations in this area occur when people overstep their authority, make decisions without proper consultation, or undermine the decisions of others. This can lead to confusion, resentment, and a lack of trust within the team.

Identifying boundary violations can often be challenging, as they can manifest as subtle behaviors or patterns that may not be immediately obvious. To recognize these violations, it is important to pay attention to signs such as consistently feeling overwhelmed or overworked, an inability to disconnect from work during personal time, feeling consistently emotionally drained or unsupported, uncomfortable or invasive interactions with colleagues, and frequent confusion or frustration surrounding decision-making processes.

Consider the following scenario, in which boundary violations are affecting the overall work environment and the well-being of an employee named Ezra. Ezra's manager, Mark, frequently assigns him tasks that go beyond his regular working hours, often with tight deadlines. Consequently, Ezra consistently stays late at the office, trying to meet these unrealistic expectations. This is an example of a time and workload boundary violation. Additionally, Mark often shares his personal problems with Ezra, expecting him to provide emotional support during work hours.

Ezra feels obligated to listen and offer help, but this emotional labor takes a toll on his mental health and leaves him emotionally drained. This is a boundary violation in the form of emotional labor. Moreover, Ezra's co-worker, Tom, has a habit of going through his personal belongings on his desk when he is away from his workspace. This invasion of privacy makes Ezra feel uncomfortable and unsafe in his work environment, constituting a privacy and personal space boundary violation. Lastly, Mark sometimes makes decisions that should involve Ezra's input, as he is responsible for certain aspects of the marketing projects.

However, he doesn't consult him, leading to confusion and frustration on Ezra's part. This is a violation of authority and decision-making boundaries. In this situation, recognizing these boundary violations is crucial for Ezra to address the issues and restore balance in his work life. By discussing his concerns with Mark and Tom, and advocating for his own well-being, Ezra can promote a more respectful and productive workplace environment. It's also essential for the organization to foster a culture that values boundaries and provides clear guidelines, ensuring that everyone understands the importance of respecting others' personal and professional limits.

Workplace culture plays a significant role in boundary violations, as it sets the tone for how you interact and relate to one another. A healthy workplace culture is one that prioritizes respect, communication, and well-being, making it less likely for boundary violations to occur. Conversely, a toxic workplace culture can enable and perpetuate these violations.

Organizations should strive to create a culture that values the importance of boundaries, providing clear expectations and guidelines for employees. This includes implementing policies that address work hours, communication, decision-making, and personal space. Additionally, cultivating a culture of open communication and feedback can empower employees to voice their concerns and address boundary violations when they arise.

Identifying and addressing boundary violations in the workplace is essential for maintaining a positive work environment and ensuring your well-being. By understanding the different types of boundary violations, recognizing subtle signs, and fostering a healthy workplace culture, you can promote a respectful and productive environment for all. This proactive approach will not only benefit you as an individual but also contribute to the overall success of the organization.

Responding to Boundary Violations

Establishing healthy boundaries is crucial for maintaining positive relationships and a sense of well-being. However, boundary violations can occur, leaving us feeling disrespected or even harmed. In such situations, it is essential to address the issue effectively and restore the balance in the relationship.

When a boundary violation occurs, it is crucial to assess whether an immediate or delayed response is appropriate. An immediate response can be beneficial when the violation is ongoing or when the situation requires prompt intervention to prevent further harm. However, in some cases, a delayed response may be more suitable, allowing both parties time to reflect and process their emotions. A delayed response can also prevent emotional outbursts, enabling a more constructive conversation.

Choosing the right communication style is critical for effectively addressing boundary violations. Three common styles include assertiveness, diplomacy, and nonviolent communication.

Assertive communication involves expressing our feelings, needs, and opinions clearly and confidently while respecting the rights and boundaries of others. It allows us to stand up for ourselves without being aggressive or confrontational. Assertiveness can be especially effective when dealing with a persistent violator who may not be responsive to gentler approaches. For example, when a co-worker repeatedly takes credit for your ideas, you might assertively say, "I appreciate your input, but I'd like to make sure that my contributions are acknowledged as well."

On the other hand, diplomatic communication involves tactfully addressing sensitive issues while maintaining a respectful and cooperative tone. Diplomacy can be useful when dealing with a situation that involves multiple parties or when the boundary violation is unintentional. It helps to foster understanding and minimize conflicts. For instance, if a friend accidentally shares personal information about you with others, you could diplomatically say, "I know you didn't mean any harm, but I would appreciate it if you could be more careful with my private information in the future."

Nonviolent communication (NVC) is another communication approach based on empathy, compassion, and understanding. NVC focuses on identifying and expressing our feelings and needs without blaming or criticizing the other person. This approach can be particularly helpful when dealing with emotionally charged situations or when the violator may not be aware of the impact of their actions. For example, if your partner has a habit of raising their voice during disagreements, you could use NVC to express your feelings: "When your voice gets loud, I feel anxious and find it difficult to listen. I need to feel safe and respected during our conversations. Could we agree to keep our voices calm when we discuss sensitive topics?"

When discussing a boundary violation with the responsible party, it is essential to follow a structured approach. Begin by objectively describing the situation and the specific behavior that constitutes the boundary violation. Avoid using judgmental language or making assumptions about the violator's intentions. Next, express your feelings and needs related to the boundary violation. Use "I" statements to take ownership of your emotions and avoid placing blame on the violator. For example, "I feel disrespected when you interrupt me during meetings."

Clearly request a change in behavior from the violator after expressing your feelings and needs. Ensure that your request is specific and reasonable. For instance, "I would appreciate it if you could wait until I finish speaking before sharing your thoughts." Finally, offer solutions to address the boundary violation and facilitate a more positive interaction in the future. This collaborative approach can foster a sense of partnership and encourage the violator to be more receptive to your concerns.

Consider Lincoln, a doctor who always set clear boundaries with his patients. He believed that open communication and respecting patients' privacy were crucial elements in fostering trust and creating a comfortable environment for them.

One day, during a session, Lincoln encountered a boundary violation. A patient named Sophia, who had been receiving treatment for a chronic condition, started to inquire about Lincoln's personal life. She began asking questions about his family, relationship status, and even his social media profiles. Initially, Lincoln attempted to redirect the conversation back to her medical concerns, but Sophia persisted with her questions.

Recognizing that an immediate response was necessary to prevent further intrusion into his personal life, Lincoln decided to use assertive communication. He calmly and confidently stated, "Sophia, I understand your curiosity, but it's important for us to maintain a professional relationship and focus on your health. My personal life is not relevant to your medical treatment."

Sophia appeared a bit taken aback, but she quickly understood the importance of respecting Lincoln's boundaries. She apologized for crossing the line and refocused the conversation on her health concerns.

By addressing the boundary violation promptly and assertively, Lincoln was able to maintain a professional relationship with Sophia while preserving his own well-being. In doing so, he ensured that his clinic remained a safe and comfortable space for both himself and his patients.

Responding to boundary violations effectively requires choosing the right timing, communication style, and addressing the issue with the violator using clear, respectful language. By following these guidelines, we can maintain healthy boundaries and preserve our well-being and relationships. As we navigate various situations in life, it is important to remember that setting and respecting boundaries are key to fostering a positive and supportive environment for everyone involved.

Strengthening and Reinforcing Boundaries

Boundaries are essential in both personal and professional settings, as they ensure that we maintain our emotional and mental well-being while fostering healthy relationships. Strengthening and reinforcing boundaries is a continuous process that requires several essential steps, such as regularly assessing and refining our boundaries, proactive communication, consistency, and follow-through, as well as enlisting support from colleagues and supervisors.

The first step in reinforcing boundaries is to continually assess and refine them. This process requires self-awareness and introspection, as we need to be in tune with our emotions and values to define our limits effectively. Regularly evaluating our boundaries allows us to recognize any changes in our needs and preferences, enabling us to adapt accordingly. This ongoing assessment ensures that our boundaries remain relevant and effective in promoting well-being and successful interactions with others.

Proactive communication is crucial in establishing and maintaining boundaries. This involves expressing our needs, preferences, and limits clearly and assertively to others, rather than waiting for boundary violations to occur. By communicating our boundaries proactively, we can prevent misunderstandings and conflicts, while fostering a culture of respect and trust. This communication should be respectful, clear, and concise, focusing on our needs rather than placing blame on others. Additionally, it is essential to listen and respond empathetically to others' boundaries, demonstrating mutual respect and understanding.

Maintaining consistency involves regularly reiterating our boundaries and ensuring that they are upheld in various situations. This persistence sends a clear message to others that our boundaries are non-negotiable and should be respected. Moreover, follow-through is the practice of addressing boundary violations immediately and assertively. Ignoring or delaying responses to boundary violations can inadvertently signal that these boundaries are flexible or unimportant. By addressing violations promptly, we can re-establish our boundaries and demonstrate the significance of respecting these limits.

Enlisting support from colleagues and supervisors can be incredibly beneficial in reinforcing boundaries. Sharing and discussing our boundaries with others can create a supportive environment where we feel validated and respected. Colleagues and supervisors can provide valuable feedback, advice, and encouragement, which can be instrumental in maintaining and strengthening our boundaries. Furthermore, supervisors can play a crucial role in reinforcing boundaries by modeling appropriate behavior, addressing boundary violations, and promoting a culture of respect. By fostering this positive environment, we are more likely to feel empowered to establish and maintain healthy boundaries.

Consider Piper, a project manager at a marketing firm. She finds herself constantly working late hours and struggling to maintain a healthy work-life balance. Piper recognizes that she needs to establish and reinforce boundaries to promote her well-being and maintain positive relationships with her colleagues.

Piper starts by reviewing and refining her personal boundaries. She reflects on her values and priorities, such as spending quality time with her family and having adequate time for self-care. She decides that she will no longer work beyond her designated hours, except in emergencies or exceptional circumstances.

Next, Piper proactively communicates her boundaries to her team members and supervisors. She explains that she will not be available for work-related discussions or tasks outside her working hours. She does so respectfully and assertively, ensuring that her needs are clear while also expressing her commitment to the team's success.

To maintain consistency, Piper regularly reiterates her boundaries during team meetings and in her email signature. She also follows through by addressing boundary violations immediately. For instance, if a colleague sends her a non-urgent work email after her designated hours, she politely reminds them of her availability and requests that they respect her boundaries.

Piper also enlists support from her colleagues and supervisors. She shares her reasons for establishing these boundaries and encourages them to do the same. Her supervisor, understanding the importance of a healthy work-life balance, supports her efforts and helps promote a culture of respect within the workplace.

As a result of Piper's proactive approach to establishing and reinforcing boundaries, she successfully regains control over her work-life balance. Her colleagues and supervisors respect her boundaries, and she feels empowered to maintain these limits. By doing so, Piper ultimately promotes her overall well-being and fosters positive relationships with her colleagues.

Strengthening and reinforcing boundaries is an ongoing process that requires self-awareness, proactive communication, consistency, follow-through, and support from others. By regularly reviewing and refining personal boundaries, we can ensure that our limits remain relevant and effective. Communicating boundaries proactively and consistently can prevent misunderstandings and promote a culture of respect, while follow-through is necessary to address boundary violations and re-establish limits. Lastly, enlisting support from colleagues and supervisors can create a supportive environment that encourages the establishment and maintenance of healthy boundaries, ultimately promoting overall well-being and positive relationships.

Preventing Future Boundary Violations

Boundary violations at work can lead to increased stress, decreased productivity, and strained relationships. However, we can prevent future boundary violations and enhance our overall satisfaction with work by taking a few proactive steps.

Firstly, it's essential for us to establish clear expectations and policies from the outset. This starts by understanding our personal values, needs, and limits. We should reflect on past experiences to identify areas where boundaries were crossed and consider what measures could have been taken to prevent those situations. By doing so, we can create guidelines that will help us navigate our professional relationships and work expectations effectively. For example, if we tend to work long hours and struggle to say no to additional tasks, we should set a clear policy for ourselves regarding our work hours and workload. We might decide to stop working at a specific time each day, and only accept new tasks if they align with our predetermined priorities.

In addition to setting expectations, promoting a healthy work culture is vital in preventing boundary violations. A healthy work culture includes fostering an environment of respect, collaboration, and support. When we feel valued and respected, we are more likely to respect the boundaries of others. One way to promote a healthy work culture is by modeling appropriate behavior. We should be mindful of how we interact with our colleagues and supervisors, and be respectful of their time and personal boundaries. For example, if we know a co-worker has family commitments in the evening, we should avoid sending non-urgent emails or making requests after their designated work hours.

Encouraging open communication and feedback is another essential component for preventing boundary violations. By fostering a culture of transparency, we feel comfortable discussing our needs and preferences, making it easier to address potential issues before they escalate. We should practice active listening and empathic responses to encourage open communication. When someone shares their concerns or preferences, we should acknowledge their feelings and show understanding. For instance, if a co-worker expresses discomfort with being contacted during weekends, we should respond with empathy and discuss ways to respect their boundaries moving forward. Additionally, we shouldn't be afraid to seek feedback from others regarding our own behavior. By doing so, we create an opportunity for growth and improvement, ultimately leading to healthier boundaries.

By taking care of ourselves physically, emotionally, and mentally, we are better equipped to recognize and enforce our boundaries. Integrating self-care into our daily routine can be as simple as taking short breaks throughout the day, practicing mindfulness techniques, or engaging in hobbies and activities that bring joy and relaxation. For example, we might consider taking a walk during our lunch break, attending a weekly yoga class, or setting aside time each evening for reading or journaling. Prioritizing self-care not only protects our well-being but also models healthy behavior for others, inspiring them to value their own well-being and respect the boundaries of their colleagues.

We can prevent future boundary violations and create a more balanced and fulfilling work environment by establishing clear expectations, fostering a healthy work culture, promoting open communication, and prioritizing self-care. Taking these proactive steps will ensure that everyone's boundaries are respected and valued.

Navigating Complex Situations

Navigating complex situations often necessitates a comprehensive understanding of power dynamics, adeptness in handling persistent or intentional boundary violators, the willingness to seek external help or resources, and the skill to evaluate when alternative options should be considered. Effectively managing these challenges is essential for establishing and maintaining healthy boundaries in various aspects of life, such as relationships, work, and social interactions.

To effectively address power dynamics, it is crucial to increase self-awareness by recognizing your position within the power structure and identifying factors contributing to that position. For example, consider your role within a team, your level of expertise, and any personal connections that may influence power dynamics. Understanding how power dynamics impact you empowers you to respond assertively and confidently. Building alliances with others in similar positions or with complementary goals can help balance power dynamics. For instance, co-workers facing similar challenges can form a support group to discuss shared concerns and strategize solutions. Collaborate with your co-workers to develop shared objectives and support each other in advocating for change. Furthermore, developing assertive communication skills allows you to communicate your boundaries and needs clearly while remaining open to the perspectives and concerns of others. This approach fosters trust and promotes mutual understanding.

Handling persistent or intentional boundary violators presents its own set of challenges. To address these, begin by clearly and assertively communicating your boundaries, explaining the reasons behind them, and outlining the consequences of continued violations. For example, if a colleague consistently interrupts your personal time, calmly explain the importance of maintaining work-life balance and inform them of your decision to disengage from work-related conversations outside of office hours. If the violator disregards your boundaries, enforce the consequences you previously detailed. This may include limiting interactions, seeking mediation, or involving an authority figure. Prioritizing self-care is crucial when dealing with persistent boundary violations. Engage in activities that promote well-being, such as exercise, meditation, or spending time with supportive friends and family.

There may come a time when alternative options need to be considered to protect your well-being. Evaluate the severity of the situation by assessing the impact of boundary violations on your mental, emotional, and physical health. If the situation is causing significant harm, it may be time to explore alternative options. Gauge the responsiveness of the violator and, if they show no willingness to respect your boundaries or engage in constructive dialogue, consider seeking alternative solutions. Assess the availability of resources and support, and determine whether you have what is necessary to navigate the situation. If not, alternative options may be more viable. Finally, weigh the potential benefits and drawbacks of pursuing alternative options, such as changing jobs, ending a relationship, or relocating. For example, consider the potential for personal growth, improved mental health, and increased stability when weighing these decisions.

By mastering these skills, you can effectively navigate complex situations and maintain healthy boundaries. The key lies in understanding power dynamics, addressing persistent or intentional violators, utilizing external resources when needed, and thoughtfully evaluating alternative options. Cultivating these skills promotes well-being and ensures that your boundaries are respected and valued.

How To Approach A Boundary Being Broken

In relationships, whether personal or professional, boundaries play a crucial role in maintaining a healthy balance and mutual respect. However, there may be instances when these boundaries are inadvertently or deliberately violated. Navigating such situations can be challenging, and knowing how to address them effectively is essential.

When a boundary is breached only once, it may not warrant an intense response. In many cases, gently reminding the other person about the boundary and its significance might suffice. For instance, if a colleague requests your assistance on a project after hours, and you have previously communicated your unavailability past a specific time, you could respond by saying, "I apologize, but I cannot stay late tonight. I have a prior commitment that I must honor." This tactful reminder can help re-establish the boundary without causing any conflict.

However, if a boundary is consistently being violated, adopting a firmer stance becomes necessary. In such cases, it is crucial to communicate your boundaries explicitly and outline your expectations from the other party. For example, if a colleague frequently asks you to engage in tasks that make you uncomfortable, you could say, "I'm sorry, but I don't feel at ease doing that. Please respect my boundaries and refrain from asking me again."

It is essential to remember that you are not obligated to justify your boundaries to anyone. Although it may be tempting to explain the reasons behind your limits, doing so could invite the other person to question or undermine your rationale. Instead, assert your boundaries confidently and anticipate that they will be respected by the other party.

One reason people continue to break boundaries is a lack of awareness or understanding. Some individuals may not be fully cognizant of the importance of personal boundaries and how their actions impact others. It is crucial to educate and inform these individuals about the significance of respecting boundaries in maintaining healthy relationships. Through open dialogue and empathy, one can help others become more aware of their actions and the consequences they may have on those around them.

Another reason for boundary violations is a disregard for the feelings or well-being of others. In some cases, individuals may prioritize their own needs and desires above those of others, leading them to breach established boundaries. It is essential to recognize and address this behavior, as it can damage relationships and undermine trust. When confronted with such behavior, it's important to remain firm in asserting your boundaries and communicating your needs. By maintaining self-respect and standing up for yourself, you can discourage further boundary violations and promote healthier interactions.

Addressing breached boundaries requires a mix of tact, assertiveness, and self-confidence. It is crucial to communicate your boundaries clearly, anticipate respect from the other party, and be prepared to enforce your limits when necessary. By fostering an environment of open communication and mutual understanding, you can establish and maintain healthy boundaries that contribute to the success and satisfaction of your personal and professional relationships. Remember that understanding why people may break boundaries can help in addressing these situations more effectively and create a stronger foundation for your relationships.

Overcoming Guilt while Establishing Boundaries

Establishing boundaries can be a daunting task for us, particularly when it demands confronting and overcoming feelings of guilt. It's entirely natural for us to experience internal conflict when we prioritize our own needs, saying "no" to others while saying "yes" to ourselves. However, we must acknowledge that any guilt we might feel is often "unearned" and not a burden we should bear.

One reason we might feel guilty when establishing boundaries is due to societal and cultural expectations that encourage us to be selfless and accommodating, often at the expense of our own well-being. Also, our past experiences, family dynamics, or personal beliefs can contribute to the development of guilt when setting boundaries. These feelings of guilt and shame can stem from a fear of disappointing others, being perceived as selfish, or even feeling unworthy of having boundaries in the first place.

In light of this, we might dread the possibility of conflict or backlash when asserting our boundaries, leading us to avoid setting them altogether. Regrettably, this avoidance can result in mounting frustration and resentment, which may prompt us to respond in a more aggressive manner. To prevent this, it's important for us to proactively set boundaries before reaching our emotional breaking point, and engage in these discussions when we're calm and collected enough to consider the other person's perspective. By approaching the situation with calmness and compassion, the individual on the receiving end will likely feel less hurt, thereby minimizing our guilt.

Recognizing the distinction between setting boundaries and being selfish is a crucial aspect of this process. We, who might have weak boundaries, often strive to "be nice" and accommodate others, even when our hearts are not genuinely in it. In contrast, those of us with healthy boundaries give out of authentic kindness and concern for others. Feeling guilty and experiencing other challenging emotions when setting boundaries is common, but it's vital to remember that this is a normal part of the process. We might feel anxious, afraid, remorseful, awkward, or ashamed, but it's important for us to push through these emotions and continue the process of setting boundaries.

As you embark on this journey, remember that establishing and maintaining boundaries is an ongoing process, requiring consistent practice and adjustment as your needs and circumstances evolve. The more you practice, the more comfortable you will become with asserting your boundaries. Developing the skill of setting boundaries effectively is a learning process that takes time, as it does not come naturally to everyone. It is crucial to understand that setting boundaries is not merely about saying "no" to others but also about saying "yes" to yourself and your well-being.

When we establish boundaries, we communicate to ourselves and others what we need and deserve, which is something to be proud of and embrace. Overcoming feelings of guilt while establishing boundaries can be challenging, but it is important to remember that these feelings are often unearned and that setting boundaries is an essential aspect of self-care and personal growth. Embrace the process, knowing it takes time and practice to become proficient in setting boundaries effectively. Keep in mind the importance of setting boundaries before reaching your emotional breaking point, differentiating between setting boundaries and being selfish, and working through challenging emotions.

Throughout this journey, remember to be patient with yourself. It is important to recognize that setbacks may occur and that you may sometimes struggle to maintain your boundaries. Use these experiences as opportunities for growth and learning, reflecting on what you could do differently in the future to better assert your needs and desires.

With time, practice, and dedication, you will become more comfortable with setting boundaries and prioritizing your well-being. As you continue to improve in this area, you will likely find that your relationships become more balanced and fulfilling, and your overall sense of self-worth and happiness will increase. Embrace the journey toward healthier boundaries and a more empowered you.

Never Apologize for Setting Strong Boundaries

A vital aspect of setting boundaries is grasping the importance of never apologizing for establishing robust and clear limits. Many of us feel the need to apologize when asserting our boundaries, fearing that we may be viewed as rude, selfish, or uncooperative. However, it's crucial to understand that setting strong boundaries is an indication of self-respect, self-awareness, and a recognition of our collective worth.

When we set strong boundaries, we are prioritizing our mental and emotional well-being, enabling us to perform at our best in all areas of life, including work. By never apologizing for our boundaries, we are sending a clear message that we value our time, energy, and contributions. This confidence can actually earn us more respect from our peers and supervisors, as they will acknowledge our commitment to maintaining a healthy work-life balance.

Refusing to apologize for setting strong boundaries encourages others to do the same, fostering a healthier and more supportive work environment for everyone. This leads to increased collaboration and improved communication among colleagues, as they can better understand each other's needs and limitations. In this manner, setting strong boundaries without apology can benefit not only our own well-being but also the overall productivity and harmony.

Establishing strong boundaries and not apologizing for them also helps us gain a sense of autonomy and control over our lives. This empowerment can have positive effects on our self-esteem and personal growth, allowing us to better comprehend our needs and desires, and make decisions aligning with our values and goals. By refusing to apologize for setting strong boundaries, we are embracing our right to chart our own course and make choices that bolster our well-being.

In situations where we might feel pressured to compromise our boundaries or apologize for them, it's important to recall why we set those boundaries in the first place. Reminding ourselves that our well-being and personal growth are non-negotiable and that by setting strong boundaries, we are investing in our long-term success and happiness is crucial. We should stand firm in our convictions and be prepared to defend our boundaries when necessary, without apology or guilt.

Incorporating the mindset of never apologizing for setting strong boundaries can be transformative in our personal and professional lives. Doing so not only takes care of us but also contributes to a healthier, more productive work environment for everyone involved. Embrace our boundaries and the self-respect that comes with them, and remember that we have every right to prioritize our well-being without apology. As we continue to set strong boundaries, we will likely find that our relationships, both at work and in our personal lives, become more balanced, fulfilling, and respectful.

As we continue to set strong boundaries and refuse to apologize for them, we'll observe several positive changes in our lives. One such change is an increased ability to manage our time effectively. When we establish clear boundaries, we have a better understanding of our limits and can allocate our time and energy accordingly. This leads to more efficient use of our resources, ultimately enabling us to achieve more in both our personal and professional lives.

Another advantage of setting strong boundaries without apology is the development of healthier relationships. When we are clear about our needs and expectations, others can better understand and respect them. This open communication and mutual respect lay the foundation for robust, supportive connections with colleagues, friends, and family members. By refusing to apologize for our boundaries, we are fostering relationships built on trust, understanding, and genuine care for each other's well-being.

Moreover, setting strong boundaries and not apologizing for them can lead to increased confidence and self-assurance. By valuing our needs and prioritizing our well-being, we send a message to ourselves that we are deserving of care, respect, and consideration. This self-validation can boost our self-esteem and empower us to take on new challenges, both in our personal lives and in our careers.

As we grow more comfortable with setting strong boundaries and standing by them without apology, we may also find that our stress levels decrease. By establishing clear limits, we can more effectively manage our workload and prevent becoming overwhelmed. This reduction in stress can have a positive impact on our overall well-being, allowing us to be more present and engaged in both our work and personal lives.

It's important to acknowledge that setting strong boundaries is not only essential for our personal well-being but can also have a significant positive impact on various aspects of our lives. By refusing to apologize for our boundaries, we are embracing our self-worth and empowering ourselves to make choices that support our long-term happiness and success. As we continue to set and maintain strong boundaries, we will likely experience increased productivity, healthier relationships, and greater overall fulfillment. We should embrace our boundaries and the benefits that come with them, and remember that we have every right to prioritize our well-being without apology.

In essence, the act of setting boundaries and standing by them without apology is an act of self-care and respect, both for ourselves and for others. It's a practice that contributes to our personal growth, strengthens our relationships, and enhances our productivity. By consistently setting and upholding these boundaries, we can foster a healthier, more balanced, and fulfilling life.

Redrawing the Line

Boundaries play a crucial role in our lives by helping us define and communicate our personal needs, desires, and limits. However, it's important to remember that boundaries are not static; they may need re-evaluation as we progress through various stages of life or as our relationships with others evolve.

One of the most telling indicators that it may be time to reassess your boundaries is if you consistently feel stressed, resentful, or exploited in your relationships. If you frequently find yourself agreeing to things you don't want to do, or if your time and energy are being drained by others, it's likely time to examine your boundaries and make appropriate adjustments. Additionally, if you notice recurring conflicts with the same individuals or have repeated arguments with co-workers and supervisors, this could signify that your boundaries are not being respected and need reinforcement.

Significant life changes, such as starting a new job, welcoming the birth of a child, or relocating to a new area, may also necessitate a re-evaluation of your boundaries. Be mindful of any major transitions or personal growth in your life, as these can impact your needs and desires. It's essential to ensure that your boundaries continue to align with your evolving priorities and values.

When reassessing your boundaries, be clear about your expectations and communicate them effectively to others. Utilize "I" statements to convey your feelings, rather than resorting to accusations or blaming others. It's equally important to be receptive to listening to others and open to finding a mutually acceptable compromise.

Setting aside time for self-reflection is another valuable strategy for re-evaluating your boundaries. Contemplate what you are willing to tolerate and what you consider unacceptable. Identifying your core values and ensuring that your boundaries align with them can provide a solid foundation for maintaining healthy relationships and a balanced life.

Boundaries are a vital component of our well-being, and it's essential to periodically assess whether they remain relevant and effective. By staying attuned to signs like persistent stress or resentment, or recurring conflicts with the same individuals, we can determine when it's time to re-examine our boundaries and make any necessary adjustments for a more harmonious life.

Boundary Evolution

Establishing and maintaining healthy boundaries is crucial for our well-being and success. We need to evaluate and adjust them over time as our lives evolve. By self-reflecting, communicating clearly, and prioritizing work-life balance, we can create a fulfilling work experience. Here are 10 ways to navigate contemporary workplace challenges with confidence.

1. **Self-Reflection:** Regularly take time to reflect on your current work boundaries, identifying areas where you feel overwhelmed, overcommitted, or undervalued. Consider what aspects of your job you genuinely enjoy and which tasks might be better delegated or renegotiated.

2. **Set Clear Expectations:** Communicate your work boundaries to colleagues, and supervisors. Establish your availability, workload capacity, and preferred communication channels. Be transparent about your expectations and open to discussing any concerns.

3. **Prioritize Work-Life Balance:** Strive to maintain a healthy balance between your professional and personal life. Set limits on working hours, be firm about taking breaks, and avoid bringing work home whenever possible. Adjust your boundaries as needed to protect your well-being.

4. **Monitor Stress Levels:** Pay attention to your stress levels and take note of situations or tasks that consistently cause tension. Reassess your boundaries in these areas and explore ways to alleviate the pressure, such as delegating tasks or seeking additional support.

5. **Establish a Support System:** Build a network of trusted colleagues who can provide guidance and feedback on your work boundaries. Share experiences and learn from one another's successes and challenges in maintaining healthy boundaries.

6. **Practice Assertiveness:** Develop assertiveness skills to communicate your boundaries effectively and respectfully. Be confident in expressing your needs and standing up for yourself when your boundaries are being tested.

7. **Embrace Flexibility:** Recognize that your boundaries may need to shift during different phases of your career or as your personal life changes. Be willing to reassess and adjust your boundaries as needed to maintain balance and fulfillment in all aspects of your life.

8. **Track Your Progress:** Regularly review your boundaries and evaluate whether they are still effective in protecting your well-being and promoting your career growth. Make adjustments as necessary and celebrate your successes in maintaining healthy work

boundaries.

9. **Seek Feedback:** Request feedback from co-workers and supervisors on how well you're maintaining your boundaries and how they impact the team. Use this feedback to refine your boundaries and improve your working relationships.

10. **Practice, practice, practice:** Practice setting and maintaining boundaries, assertiveness, and time management. Continuously develop your skills to better manage your work boundaries over time.

By implementing these strategies, you can develop and maintain healthy boundaries that adapt to your changing needs and circumstances. Remember to stay vigilant, communicate your boundaries effectively, and prioritize your mental and physical health as you navigate the complexities of the modern work environment.

The Triumph of Managing Boundaries

In conclusion, navigating through life, setting healthy boundaries is crucial for our emotional, psychological, and social well-being. Boundaries act as invisible lines that define our limits and govern our interactions with others. They enable us to maintain a sense of self, protect our emotional and physical space, and foster harmonious relationships.

Boundary violations occur when our limits are disregarded, leading to feelings of discomfort, resentment, or even violation. These transgressions can stem from a lack of awareness or intentional manipulation by others. Managing boundary violations involves recognizing these transgressions, asserting our limits, and nurturing self-respect. By consistently asserting our boundaries, we cultivate a strong sense of self-worth, which serves as a foundation for personal growth and fulfillment.

In the long run, a healthy self-esteem allows us to confidently navigate the world and make decisions that align with our values and priorities. Additionally, managing boundary infringements can help reduce the emotional turmoil that results from feeling disrespected or mistreated. This mental clarity allows us to focus on our goals and aspirations, making it easier to achieve personal and professional success.

Moreover, setting and respecting boundaries fosters a sense of trust and mutual respect in relationships. This open communication allows us to engage in genuine, authentic connections with others, deepening our interpersonal bonds and promoting emotional well-being. Addressing boundary violations can also help us to assertively address conflicts as they arise, preventing resentment from festering and growing. This proactive approach to conflict resolution promotes healthy communication and understanding, ultimately strengthening our relationships.

Healthy boundaries play a significant role in both personal and professional growth. In our personal lives, they enable us to establish our identity and prioritize our needs and values. They provide a framework for understanding our emotions and behaviors, which is essential for self-improvement. By consistently evaluating and adjusting our boundaries, we can evolve and grow as individuals, nurturing our emotional intelligence and interpersonal skills.

In a professional context, healthy boundaries allow us to maintain a balance between our work and personal lives. They ensure that we dedicate adequate time and energy to both domains, preventing burnout and fostering sustainable success. Furthermore, the ability to set and maintain boundaries in the workplace demonstrates emotional intelligence, assertiveness, and effective communication, which are essential skills for career advancement.

As we encounter new experiences and challenges, our boundaries may need to shift and evolve. Being open to re-evaluating and adjusting our limits fosters adaptability and resilience, allowing us to navigate change and overcome obstacles with grace and confidence.

Managing boundary violations and cultivating healthy boundaries is essential for our overall well-being and personal and professional growth. By recognizing and addressing boundary infringements, we can improve our self-esteem, reduce stress and anxiety, enhance our relationships, and effectively resolve conflicts. Moreover, healthy boundaries provide a foundation for self-improvement, professional success, and the development of essential life skills, such as adaptability and resilience. Ultimately, by prioritizing our boundaries, we can thrive and flourish in all aspects of life.

Self-Assessment - Managing Boundary Violations

Boundaries are an essential part of personal and professional life, establishing a healthy balance between individual well-being and group dynamics. As we navigate our way through varying environments, it's important to reflect upon our ability to manage boundaries effectively. This self-assessment is designed to help you gauge your skills and resilience in managing boundary violations, a key aspect that can influence not just your professional success, but also your mental health and overall well-being.

Please read each statement carefully and rate your agreement using the following scale:

1 = Strongly Disagree 2 = Disagree 3 = Neutral 4 = Agree 5 = Strongly Agree

1. I can easily identify when my boundaries have been violated at work.
2. I am confident in my ability to address boundary violations when they occur.
3. I have a clear understanding of the steps I should take to respond to boundary violations.
4. I proactively communicate my boundaries to others to minimize the risk of violations.
5. I am able to remain assertive and composed when addressing boundary violations.
6. I have a support system (colleagues, friends, or family) I can turn to when dealing with boundary violations.
7. I am able to recognize patterns in boundary violations and take proactive steps to prevent them.
8. I reassess my boundaries periodically to ensure they are still effective and relevant.

9. I seek constructive feedback from trusted colleagues to help me understand potential boundary issues.
10. I am open to adjusting my boundaries if a situation warrants a change.
11. I have established clear consequences for boundary violations and effectively communicate them.
12. I am capable of navigating complex situations involving boundary violations without compromising my well-being.
13. I can identify the root causes of boundary violations and address them accordingly.
14. I am able to maintain a healthy balance between asserting my boundaries and maintaining positive relationships.
15. I have successfully resolved situations involving breached boundaries in the past.
16. I do not feel guilty when enforcing my boundaries, even when they have been violated.
17. I am comfortable seeking guidance from supervisors or HR when faced with persistent boundary violations.
18. I recognize the importance of self-care and mental health when dealing with boundary violations.
19. I use my past experiences with boundary violations as learning opportunities to strengthen my boundaries in the future.
20. I am committed to maintaining a healthy work environment by effectively managing boundary violations.

Interpretation

Add up your total score and refer to the following scale:

20-40: You may need to work on recognizing, addressing, and managing boundary violations more effectively. Consider seeking guidance and support from trusted colleagues or professionals to help you develop these skills.

41-60: You have some awareness of boundary violations and are developing strategies to manage them. Continue to work on improving your skills, seeking feedback, and learning from your experiences.

61-80: You have a good understanding of boundary violations and how to manage them. Keep refining your skills, seeking feedback, and maintaining your boundaries in the workplace.

81-100: You excel at managing boundary violations and maintaining a healthy work environment. Continue to be proactive in enforcing your boundaries and providing support to others who may be struggling with similar issues.

Managing boundary violations is a complex process that requires self-awareness, effective communication, and resilience. Reflecting on this assessment should provide you with valuable insights into your strengths and areas for development in this crucial area. Remember, boundaries are not static; they are dynamic and should be reviewed and adjusted as needed to ensure you maintain a healthy and respectful work environment.

Exercise: Managing Boundary Violations

1. Reflect on a recent situation where your work boundaries were violated. How did you react? What could you have done differently to assert your boundaries more effectively?
2. What steps can you take in the next week to make your work boundaries clearer to others? How will you ensure they are respected?
3. What proactive measures can you implement to prevent future boundary violations at work? Consider both verbal and non-verbal cues.
4. Can you think of a complex situation at work where maintaining your boundaries was challenging? How did you navigate it? Looking back, would you handle it differently now?
5. Suppose a respected colleague or manager crosses one of your boundaries. How would you approach this situation? What

language would you use to express your feelings and re-establish the boundary?

6. Do you feel guilty when setting boundaries at work? Why? How can you work on releasing this guilt and understanding that boundaries are essential for your well-being?

7. Have you ever felt the need to apologize for setting a boundary at work? How can you shift your mindset to understand that strong boundaries are a sign of self-respect and professionalism, not a cause for apology?

8. How do you know when it's time to re-evaluate your boundaries with work? What are some signs that your current boundaries are no longer serving you?

9. What strategies have you employed in the past to manage boundary violations? Which were successful, and which were not? How can you build upon this experience to manage future violations more effectively?

10. What proactive measures can you take to prevent future boundary violations?

11. How do you maintain your boundaries during difficult conversations at work? How might you improve your approach?

12. How can you ensure that you are respecting the boundaries of others while maintaining your own? What strategies can you use to balance these sometimes conflicting needs?

Chapter 10: Boundary Setting and Self-Awareness

"No boundary can stand strong without the pillar of self-awareness."

– Jonathan Riley

The Journey to Self-Discovery

Our journey to self-discovery is as much about understanding our limits as it is about exploring our potential. It is, in essence, a journey towards achieving a delicate balance between these two facets of our being. This equilibrium is attained by setting boundaries, an act that mirrors our self-awareness and reflects our aspirations, values, and needs. This chapter, therefore, is devoted to setting the stage for a profound exploration of boundaries and self-awareness, unveiling their power, and understanding their role in empowering us to become the best versions of ourselves.

Boundaries are not merely metaphorical lines drawn in the sand. They are an essential construct of our identity, defining our personal space, and shaping our interactions with the world around us. They serve as a beacon, guiding us through life's many complexities. However, to set effective boundaries, we must first embark on the journey to self-discovery, as it is only through understanding ourselves that we can truly comprehend where and when these lines need to be drawn.

Setting boundaries can often seem daunting. We fear being perceived as selfish or inconsiderate. But in reality, boundaries are an expression of self-respect and self-care. They signal a profound understanding of our emotional, mental, and physical needs, and, importantly, the courage to prioritize them. Boundaries, in their essence, are an act of self-love. To set them is to stand in our truth, displaying an inherent awareness of our self-worth.

Unveiling the power of boundaries allows us to understand their transformative potential. They are not barriers, but rather bridges connecting us to our authentic selves. Boundaries allow us to live in alignment with our beliefs, to engage with others respectfully, and to foster meaningful relationships. They endow us with the ability to say no when we need to, to step back when we must, and to step forward when we're ready. They enable us to navigate the complexities of life with a sense of dignity and grace, empowering us to live a life that resonates with who we are at our core.

This understanding serves as a prelude to empowerment. A deep awareness of our boundaries infuses us with a sense of control over our lives. It allows us to create a safe space for ourselves, where we can grow, learn, and thrive. It endows us with a sense of security and certainty, even amidst life's unpredictable twists and turns. It empowers us to take ownership of our journey, steering it in a direction that aligns with our values, aspirations, and needs.

The interplay of boundaries and self-awareness is a fascinating dance of the self. Boundaries are, in essence, a manifestation of our self-awareness. Our ability to set and maintain them reflects our understanding of our needs, our limitations, our strengths, and our vulnerabilities. It mirrors our understanding of who we are and what we value. Conversely, each time we set a boundary, it deepens our self-awareness, shedding light on aspects of ourselves that we may not have previously recognized or acknowledged.

Setting boundaries and being self-aware is a journey, not a destination. It is a continuous process of self-discovery, self-reflection, and self-growth. As we journey through life, our boundaries will evolve, and so will our self-awareness. Each experience, each interaction, each decision will provide us with valuable insights, nudging us closer to a deeper understanding of ourselves and the world around us.

The Role of Self-Awareness in Setting Boundaries

The human psyche is akin to a grand labyrinth, rich with complexities and nuances. At the heart of this labyrinth lie our boundaries, invisible yet potent lines that delineate our personal and emotional spaces, guarding our values, and overall wellbeing. These boundaries, while vital, are not self-generating. They require an inner compass, a guiding light to shape and define them. This beacon of illumination is our self-awareness, the introspective understanding of our inner selves, which is the foundational cornerstone of our personal development.

Self-awareness is more than just a psychological buzzword. It's an interactive process through which we perceive our emotions, motivations, desires, and the very essence of who we are. This self-perception acts as a blueprint for our boundaries. Every piece of understanding we gather about ourselves, every revelation about our emotional responses, our likes and dislikes, our values and beliefs, contributes to this blueprint. It's akin to the architect's initial sketches before building a house, providing an outline that guides the construction of our boundaries.

One of the most potent tools in our self-awareness arsenal is introspection. Through introspection, we dive deep into our emotional waters, exploring the depths of our thoughts, feelings, and reactions. It uncovers our authentic self, unmasking our strengths and weaknesses, our passions, and our fears. This knowledge, this introspective power, is fundamental in establishing robust personal and professional boundaries. For instance, when we understand our emotional triggers, we can establish boundaries to shield us from situations that cause unnecessary stress or discomfort.

Self-awareness also plays a pivotal role in unleashing our potential, pushing us beyond our self-imposed limitations and encouraging personal growth. It's like using an internal mirror to reflect our true selves. Every time we consult this mirror, we gain a clearer picture of who we are and who we aspire to be. This iterative process of self-reflection and self-understanding gradually refines our boundaries, ensuring they become more attuned to our authentic self with each cycle.

However, the intersection of self-awareness and boundaries is not a linear process. It's a complex, dynamic crossroad where internal and external influences continually reshape our limits. Our evolving perspectives, changing tolerance levels, and shifting values continuously redefine what's acceptable and what's not. This evolution mandates a constant reassessment and realignment of our boundaries, making self-awareness an ongoing journey rather than a one-time quest.

Harnessing this inner strength and using it to set, maintain, and adjust our boundaries, leads to a healthier and more balanced life. It enhances our capacity to assertively express our needs and wants, to say 'no' when necessary and 'yes' when it aligns with our values. It allows us to protect our energy and time, preventing emotional drain and burnout, and above all, it empowers us to stand our ground, reinforcing our autonomy and self-respect.

Mastering the balance between self-awareness and boundary setting is a skill that necessitates practice, patience, and perseverance. It involves continuous introspection, effective communication, and a deep respect for one's self and others. It's about understanding our worth, ensuring that our boundaries accurately reflect it, and that it is recognized and respected by others.

As we become more attuned to our inner selves, our boundaries begin to reflect this deeper understanding. We may find that we tolerate less of what depletes us and invite more of what nourishes us. The boundaries we set based on our increased self-awareness become a source of empowerment, a testament to our growth and evolution.

But, it's important to remember that the path to mastering self-awareness and boundary setting is not always smooth. There will be challenges, misunderstandings, and even resistance, both from within ourselves and from others. At such times, it's critical to draw strength from our self-awareness, to remember why we set these boundaries in the first place. The journey may be arduous, but each step, each boundary defined and upheld, brings us closer to a life of authenticity, respect, and fulfillment.

The role of self-awareness in setting boundaries is indisputably crucial. It provides the blueprint, the mirror for introspection, and the inner strength required to establish and uphold our personal and professional limits. It is the cornerstone of a balanced life, a life in which our needs, wants, and values are respected and fulfilled.

Understanding Your Limits and Strengths

The journey to self-awareness begins with the understanding of your limits and strengths. Picture a sailboat on a vast sea. Your strengths are the sturdy hull that keeps the ship afloat, and your limits are the sails that catch the wind. Without a strong hull or well-set sails, the ship risks capsizing or being blown off course. In this metaphor, self-awareness is the compass that guides the ship, ensuring safe navigation through both calm and turbulent waters.

This journey requires a keen understanding of your unique spectrum of abilities, which spans your most compelling strengths to your most evident limitations. Each person is a complex mosaic of talents, skills, weaknesses, and limitations. This spectrum is not static but rather a dynamic and evolving entity. It's shaped by our experiences, values, beliefs, and personal growth. Deciphering your limits and strengths isn't about comparing yourself to others; it's about gaining a deeper understanding of your unique spectrum. This process requires introspection, self-discovery, patience, humility, and above all, honesty.

Acknowledging limits and harnessing strengths may seem contradictory, but they are two sides of the same coin. Our society often glorifies the idea of limitless potential, which can obscure the importance of recognizing and respecting our inherent limitations. However, acknowledging our limits is not an admission of defeat. Instead, it's an act of self-awareness and self-care. Understanding our boundaries allows us to focus our efforts where they are most effective, protect our wellbeing, and prevent undue stress or burnout.

At the same time, harnessing strengths is about celebrating what we excel at. It's about recognizing our innate talents and skills and putting them to use in meaningful ways. This doesn't mean we ignore our weaknesses or cease striving to improve. Instead, it means we leverage our strengths as powerful tools for personal and professional growth. Harnessing strengths helps us build resilience, overcome challenges, and contribute positively to our relationships and communities.

The navigation between limits and strengths is a delicate balancing act, a dance, if you will. In this dance, the awareness and acceptance of our limits form one step, while the recognition and utilization of our strengths form the other. We move forward by rhythmically alternating between these steps, always mindful of our personal spectrum and continually adjusting our movements to maintain balance. This dance is a testament to self-awareness and serves as the bedrock of effective boundary setting.

Your strengths and limits are not disparate entities but are deeply interconnected, shaping your identity from the inside out. Grasping your inner strengths involves understanding what fuels your passion, what areas you naturally excel in, and where you feel most competent. It's about recognizing the parts of you that shine brightly and using them to illuminate your path.

Recognizing your limits, conversely, involves understanding what depletes you, where you struggle, and where you need support or growth. It's about acknowledging the parts of you that need nurturing, patience, and understanding, and providing the space for them to grow and evolve.

A crucial aspect of understanding your strengths and limits is practicing self-compassion. It's easy to judge ourselves harshly when we encounter our limits, but self-compassion allows us to acknowledge our limitations without self-condemnation. It fosters resilience and personal growth by providing a safe space to learn, grow, and evolve. Similarly, when utilizing our strengths, it's essential not to become complacent, but rather to use our strengths as a platform for continuous learning and growth.

Setting boundaries and self-awareness are not about erecting walls or distancing ourselves from others. Instead, they're about establishing a personal compass that guides us through life. They are about knowing where your unique spectrum of strengths and limits lies and navigating life with this self-knowledge at the forefront. Self-awareness is a continuous journey, not a destination. Each step you take along this path, each moment of introspection and acknowledgment, brings you closer to a more authentic and fulfilling life.

Identifying Your Personal Values and Goals

In the quest for personal fulfillment and authentic living, identifying your core values and goals serves as a pivotal step. These elements act as the lifeblood of your identity, the DNA of your aspirations, and the blueprint of your existence. They are the inner compass that guides you, even when the fog of indecision or uncertainty cloaks your path.

The journey begins by setting healthy boundaries, particularly in your professional life. Work-life balance isn't a luxury; it's an essential part of sustaining your emotional, mental, and physical well-being. When you understand your values and goals, you'll be able to establish boundaries that protect your time, energy, and focus. However, it's not about rigidly compartmentalizing your life. Instead, it's about creating space for growth and fulfillment in every aspect of your existence.

Uncovering your core values is a process of introspection and self-exploration. It involves peeling back the layers of societal expectations, external influences, and internalized beliefs that may not truly align with who you are or who you aspire to be. This process requires courage, as it involves questioning the status quo and challenging the structures that may have been imposed upon you. It's about finding the values that resonate with your authentic self—the ones that, when honored, bring a sense of harmony and peace.

Your core values could range from integrity to creativity, from compassion to ambition. They are unique to you and reflect your essence. Once these core values are identified, they become the guiding principles in your life, informing your decisions, shaping your reactions, and influencing your goals.

Identifying your personal goals and aspirations is the next significant step. These are the milestones that you wish to achieve, the dreams that you yearn to realize, and the legacy that you want to leave. These goals are the tangible manifestations of your core values, and they provide direction and purpose to your life.

However, simply identifying your values and goals isn't enough. You must also ensure that your boundaries align with them. This means consciously setting limits that respect your values and support your goals. It means saying 'no' when work encroaches upon your personal time, or choosing not to engage in relationships that don't honor your values. It's about making choices that affirm your worth and reflect your commitment to living authentically.

In essence, your boundaries become the guardians of your values and goals. They ensure that your actions and decisions align with your inner compass. They protect you from external pressures that might steer you off course. They provide a framework for managing your responsibilities and prioritizing your needs.

In search of authenticity, defining your values and goals is just the beginning. The true challenge lies in living them out every day, in every decision you make. It's about staying true to yourself amidst the noise and chaos of the world. It's about having the courage to say 'yes' to what aligns with your values and 'no' to what doesn't. It's about setting boundaries that preserve your energy, protect your time, and promote your well-being.

Remember, this process isn't a one-time event but a continuous journey of self-discovery and growth. As you evolve, your values might deepen, your goals might shift, and your boundaries might need adjusting. That's perfectly okay. What matters is that you stay connected with your inner compass, keep clarifying your values, and keep setting goals that reflect your authentic self.

Self-Reflection Exercises for Better Boundary Setting

Boundaries, those invisible lines that delineate our personal space physically, emotionally, and mentally, are integral to our wellbeing. However, identifying, setting, and maintaining them is an ongoing process that requires deep self-reflection and constant inward journeying.

Self-reflection exercises are the bedrock of better boundary setting. Start with a simple journaling exercise that helps you identify your current boundaries. Write down instances in your daily life where you felt uncomfortable, drained, or disrespected. These feelings often signal crossed boundaries. Be honest with yourself in this exercise. It will illuminate areas where your boundaries need to be strengthened and the types of situations or people that tend to cross them.

Next, engage in a self-reflection exercise called the "boundary visualization". Close your eyes and visualize a space that you feel most comfortable in. Imagine a boundary around this space. What does it look like? What is it made of? How does it feel to be within this boundary? This exercise helps you mentally construct what your ideal boundary would look like, equipping you with a clearer vision of what you want to achieve.

Tools for transformation come in many forms, and in this context, one of the most potent tools is the "three-step boundary setting" method. This involves acknowledging, asserting, and acting. Acknowledge your feelings when a boundary has been crossed. Assert your boundary by communicating it clearly to the individual involved. Act by consistently upholding your boundary even when it is challenged. This tool transforms your self-awareness into actionable steps towards healthier boundaries.

Inward journey exercises are also essential to enhancing boundary setting. The "past-present-future" exercise involves looking at your history of boundary setting, assessing your present boundaries, and envisioning your future boundaries. Reflect on why you've allowed certain boundaries to be crossed in the past and how you can prevent this from happening in the future. This exercise allows you to journey within and uncover the root causes of your boundary issues, thus paving the way for effective boundary setting.

Self-reflection activities for improved boundaries often involve externalizing your thoughts. Try the "boundary role-play" activity. Enlist a trusted friend or mentor and simulate scenarios where your boundaries are being tested. Practice asserting your boundaries within these scenarios. This role-play can provide invaluable insights into your boundary-setting habits and offer real-time feedback for improvement.

Mindful self-reflection exercises for stronger boundaries integrate mindfulness into the process. The "mindful boundary scan" is a practice where you sit quietly, take deep breaths, and scan your body and mind for any signs of discomfort or tension. These feelings could signal a crossed boundary. By cultivating awareness of these signs, you can address boundary issues as they arise.

The "gazing inward" practical exercise takes you deeper into your internal world. It involves creating a "boundary mantra", a personal phrase that embodies your commitment to maintaining your boundaries. It could be as simple as "I respect and uphold my boundaries" or referring to our rights. Repeat this mantra daily. It serves as a constant reminder of your commitment and a tool to reinforce your boundary setting.

The journey to better boundary setting starts with self-reflection and inward journeying. Through these exercises - journaling, boundary visualization, the three-step boundary setting method, past-present-future exercise, boundary role-play, mindful boundary scan, and the boundary mantra - you're equipped with practical tools to create, uphold, and respect your boundaries. Remember, these are not one-time exercises but ongoing practices that evolve as you do.

Building Emotional Intelligence for Effective Boundaries

In the intricate tapestry of human interaction, boundaries play a pivotal role. They act as the invisible lines that define our personal comfort zones, setting the parameters for our relationships. Building Emotional Intelligence (EI) can significantly enhance our ability to establish these boundaries effectively, going beyond the realm of traditional IQ.

Emotional Intelligence, often misunderstood as an ambiguous notion, is a powerful tool that can be harnessed to improve our interpersonal relationships and personal well-being. It comprises four key elements: self-awareness, self-management, social awareness, and relationship management. Together, these components can foster a healthy understanding of our own emotions and those of others, a crucial aspect of setting boundaries.

The process of boundary setting is intrinsically linked to self-awareness, the foundational stone of Emotional Intelligence. Self-awareness is a voyage into the inner recesses of our emotional landscape, a journey that allows us to identify, understand, and respect our feelings. By attuning ourselves to our emotional state, we can decipher our needs and limits more clearly, which in turn helps us draw effective boundaries.

Self-management, another integral facet of EI, empowers us to regulate our emotions, handle stress, and adapt to changing circumstances. It plays a crucial role in maintaining the boundaries we've established. Let's say a close friend repeatedly crosses a personal boundary, causing distress. Here, self-management enables us to control our emotional response, communicate our feelings calmly, and reinforce our boundary.

Enhancing Boundary Setting through Emotional Intelligence requires not just an understanding of our emotions, but also a sensitivity towards others' feelings. This is where social awareness comes in. This facet of EI allows us to perceive, interpret, and react to the emotions of those around us. It equips us with the ability to navigate social dynamics adeptly, respecting others' boundaries while making ours known.

Relationship management, the final component of EI, guides us in managing interactions with others positively. It enables us to resolve conflicts, influence others, and maintain healthy relationships, all while respecting and enforcing our boundaries.

Strengthening Boundaries with Emotional Intelligence hinges on the ability to express our emotions openly and assertively. For instance, instead of saying "You're making me upset," which implies that the other person controls your feelings, try "I feel upset when...". This approach, rooted in emotional intelligence, emphasizes personal responsibility for one's feelings and strengthens the boundary-setting process.

The Role of Emotional Intelligence in Setting Boundaries underscores that the ability to establish and maintain boundaries isn't solely dependent on cognitive intelligence. IQ may enable us to comprehend, analyze, and reason, but it falls short when it comes to understanding the nuanced emotions that drive human behavior.

Emotional Intelligence, however, equips us with the necessary tools to navigate these emotional complexities. It enables us to recognize when our boundaries are being infringed upon, and communicate our discomfort effectively. It allows us to respect the boundaries of others, promoting mutual understanding and fostering healthier relationships.

Emotional Intelligence serves as a compass guiding us in the establishment and maintenance of our boundaries. It goes beyond cognitive intelligence, delving into the realm of emotions to help us understand ourselves and others better. Building, enhancing, and strengthening our boundaries through Emotional Intelligence paves the way for healthier, more respectful, and fulfilling relationships, underscoring the importance of emotional acuity in the tapestry of human interaction.

Advocate for a Healthy Work Environment

In the pursuit of progress and productivity, the modern workplace often falls prey to a culture of relentless drive, a relentless drive that paradoxically often leads to a decline in both employee health and organizational productivity. An imbalanced workspace, characterized by unsustainable work hours, high-stress environments, and neglect of employee wellbeing, breeds discontent, burnout, and turnover - factors detrimental to the collective success of any enterprise. In response to this ubiquitous issue, the imperative to advocate for a healthier workspace has never been more pressing.

Advocacy in the workplace is not a luxury, but a necessity. It is a strategic advantage, providing the leverage needed to shift from a culture of mere survival to one of thriving, ensuring the welfare of individual employees while fostering a robust, resilient, and productive organization. Advocacy is the voice that champions the needs and concerns of workers, thereby empowering them to perform at their best, nourishing both their personal growth and the organization's bottom line.

In advocating for a healthier workspace, we engage in a two-pronged approach: we address the systemic issues of the work environment and promote personal strategies for maintaining balance and wellbeing. On a systemic level, this involves championing flexible work schedules, promoting regular breaks, and encouraging mental health days - recognizing that productivity is not a product of relentless grind, but of balanced, sustainable effort. At the same time, we must emphasize the importance of personal responsibility in maintaining this balance: proper nutrition, regular exercise, and adequate rest are all crucial components of a healthy work-life balance.

One of the most potent weapons in the advocacy arsenal is dialogue. Open communication between all levels of an organization can illuminate the issues that often lurk in the shadows. Leaders who listen, who genuinely seek to understand the experiences and struggles of their team, are more equipped to make changes that foster a healthier work environment. When employees feel heard, they not only gain a sense of empowerment but also a deeper sense of loyalty to the organization.

Moreover, it's essential to advocate for a culture of respect and inclusion, where diverse perspectives are valued and everyone feels that they belong. Respectful work environments reduce stress and conflict, contributing to both individual and collective wellbeing. Such environments are built on mutual trust, understanding, and acceptance, qualities that must be actively cultivated and reinforced.

Training is another crucial aspect of advocacy. By equipping employees with knowledge about stress management, mindfulness techniques, and the importance of setting boundaries, they can better navigate the challenges of the work environment. Similarly, training managers to recognize signs of burnout and to encourage their teams to take breaks and prioritize wellbeing can have a transformative effect on the work culture.

Lastly, advocacy should extend to the physical environment. A workspace that prioritizes physical health - with ergonomically designed furniture, access to natural light, and areas for relaxation and movement - can significantly improve employee wellbeing and productivity.

Advocating for a healthier workspace is not a single action, but a continuous process. It is about creating a culture where we feel valued, heard, and cared for, where wellbeing is not an afterthought but a central consideration. It is about recognizing that healthy employees are not only more productive, but more creative, more engaged, and more resilient. In our pursuit of a balanced workspace, advocacy is not just an advantage, it is an absolute necessity - a stand we must take to ensure the health and success of our organizations.

Periodic Boundary Check-Ins

Boundaries are important in interpersonal dynamics because they define personal space, comfort, and respect. They are essentially a manifestation of our individuality, delineating where one person ends and another begins. Yet, the maintenance and nurturing of these invisible barriers require vigilant effort, underscoring the importance of periodic boundary check-ins.

Periodic boundary check-ins serve as a touchstone, a recurring point of reference in the tumultuous sea of relationships. These check-ins are not merely reminders but navigational tools, steering the course of interpersonal interactions towards respect and understanding. They involve conscious and deliberate efforts to revisit the set boundaries, allowing for open communication and adjustment according to the shifts in our lives and relationships.

Keeping boundaries in check is much like tending a garden. Just as plants need regular watering, pruning, and care to thrive, so do the boundaries we set. They need to be revisited, reassessed, and sometimes, readjusted. Each check-in allows for a wholesome evaluation of the set limits, allowing us to discern if they still serve their intended purpose or if they require modification to accommodate evolving circumstances.

A pertinent question here would be, why is keeping boundaries in check so crucial? The answer lies in the very nature of human relationships. Relationships are dynamic, ever-evolving entities, reflecting the changing facets of individual identities and shared experiences. As we grow and evolve, so do our needs, comfort zones, and tolerance levels. What was acceptable a year ago might not be so today. Hence, without regular check-ins, our boundaries might either become obsolete or overly rigid, hindering the natural flow of relationships.

The role of regular check-ins extends beyond maintaining boundaries. It is a practice of self-care, of acknowledging and respecting our emotional and mental space. It also fosters trust and understanding in relationships, as it necessitates open communication and mutual agreement. It is a shared understanding that both parties are willing to respect and uphold the established boundaries, enhancing the overall health of the relationship.

Boundaries, however, are not merely about setting limits but also about allowing a certain degree of flexibility. Life is full of unexpected turns, and relationships are no exception. There are times when existing boundaries may need to be loosened, and others when they may need to be tightened. Regular check-ins provide the platform for such adjustments, ensuring that the boundaries remain relevant and effective.

"Stay on course," is a phrase often used in navigational contexts, but it also holds relevance when discussing boundaries. Just as a ship needs constant adjustments to stay on course amidst changing winds and currents, so do our boundaries in the face of shifting personal and relational dynamics. Periodic check-ins are our compass and rudder in this ongoing journey, helping us maintain a steady course while accommodating the necessary deviations.

In the end, periodic boundary check-ins are about balance and respect. They are about acknowledging that while we have a shared space in our relationships, we also have individual territories that need to be respected. Regular check-ins ensure that the balance between these shared and individual spaces is maintained, allowing for a harmonious co-existence.

They are an exercise in respect, both for oneself and for the other, nurturing a culture of mutual understanding and empathy.

Therefore, the importance of these check-ins cannot be overstated. They are the checkpoints in our journey of relationships, the lighthouses guiding us through the ebbs and flows of interpersonal dynamics. They are not just about maintaining boundaries but about fostering growth, understanding, and respect in our relationships, making them an indispensable tool in the art of boundary management.

Celebrating Successes and Learning from Setbacks

In the realm of personal development, the ongoing dance between boundaries, triumphs, and transformations often becomes the rhythm of our growth cycle. In this journey, we learn to cherish our achievements while treating our setbacks not as catastrophes but as invaluable lessons. Celebrating successes and learning from setbacks is not just an approach, it is an art.

Embracing successes in boundary setting is a powerful means of validating our strength, resilience, and courage. Every time we stand firm, articulate our needs, and maintain our boundaries, we move a step closer towards self-actualization. We may not always recognize it, but every success—no matter how minor it may seem—contributes to the shaping of our self-esteem and self-efficacy.

Yet, the path to personal growth is rarely a straight, unobstructed one. It is woven with intricate threads of triumphs and transformations, alongside inevitable challenges. Learning to accept and grow from setbacks is a crucial part of this journey. When we stumble, it is an invitation to introspect, reassess our strategies, and readjust our approach. Each misstep can offer a powerful lesson, a chance to strengthen our resilience and our resolve.

Consider the growth cycle as a natural ebb and flow between milestones and missteps. When we celebrate progress, we're not just acknowledging the endpoint, but the entirety of the journey – the effort, the dedication, the resilience that got us there. The successes become markers of our capacity to grow and adapt, to uphold our boundaries even when it seems most challenging.

However, learning from failures is equally significant. Each setback uncovers a hidden facet of our resilience, a testament to our ability to bounce back stronger. These experiences offer us insights into our boundary-setting strategies, allowing us to identify what works and what needs refining. By viewing setbacks not as failures, but as opportunities for growth, we can transform our perception of these events, fostering resilience and encouraging perseverance.

It is in this dance of celebration and learning that we find our rhythm, our unique pattern of growth. By acknowledging successes and setbacks, we adopt an integrated approach that fosters balance and harmony. We learn to celebrate achievements not as isolated victories, but as affirmations of our growth. Meanwhile, we view challenges not as insurmountable obstacles, but as stepping stones on our journey towards self-realization.

At the core of this process is the ability to bounce back and move forward, a resilience that stems from our commitment to personal growth and boundary setting. This resilience is our safety net, catching us when we falter, and propelling us forward when we triumph. It's the driving force that allows us to recognize our successes, learn from our setbacks, and continually strive for better.

As we celebrate achievements and learn from challenges, we engage in a cycle of constant evolution, a process marked by triumph and transformation. It's a cycle that encourages us not just to aim for success, but to embrace the journey in its entirety, setbacks and all. By doing so, we can truly appreciate the intricate tapestry of our personal growth, woven with threads of success, resilience, setbacks, and learning.

Ultimately, boundary setting is not merely about defining our limits; it is about understanding ourselves, our capacities, our resilience, and our potential for growth. As we navigate this journey, celebrating successes and learning from setbacks becomes a testament to our resilience, a celebration of our evolution, and a triumphant affirmation of our transformation.

Self-Assessment - Boundary Setting and Self-Awareness

Boundaries are an integral aspect of personal and professional life, shaping how we interact with others and defining our own sense of self. This self-assessment explores my ability to establish and manage these boundaries, whilst also shedding light on my self-awareness and its role in this process. The purpose of this assessment is not only to understand my current standing but also to identify areas for future improvement and growth.

For each statement, rate how strongly you agree or disagree on a scale from 1 to 5, where 1 is "strongly disagree" and 5 is "strongly agree."

1. I am aware of my personal values and how they influence my boundary-setting process.
2. I am conscious of my strengths and limitations when it comes to setting boundaries.
3. I consistently practice self-reflection to better understand and adjust my boundaries.
4. I recognize the importance of emotional intelligence in establishing and maintaining effective boundaries.
5. I actively advocate for a healthy work environment that respects and upholds boundaries.
6. I am confident in my ability to set and communicate my boundaries with others.
7. I regularly evaluate my boundaries to ensure they align with my personal values and goals.
8. I take responsibility for my well-being and prioritize self-care in my boundary-setting efforts.
9. I make an effort to learn from setbacks and celebrate successes in my boundary-setting journey.
10. I am comfortable saying "no" when necessary to protect my boundaries.
11. I acknowledge and respect the boundaries of others in the

workplace.

12. I effectively handle boundary violations and take steps to prevent future breaches.

13. I use assertive communication techniques to express my boundaries clearly and confidently.

14. I adjust my boundaries as needed to maintain a healthy work-life balance.

15. I am aware of how my emotional state affects my ability to set and maintain boundaries.

16. I seek feedback from trusted colleagues or supervisors to ensure my boundaries are appropriate and respected.

17. I understand the importance of balancing flexibility and firmness in my boundary-setting efforts.

18. I am committed to continuous self-improvement and self-awareness in my boundary-setting journey.

19. I recognize the role of self-awareness in setting effective boundaries and actively work on enhancing my self-awareness.

20. I believe that setting healthy boundaries contributes to my overall well-being and professional success.

Interpretation

Add up your total score and refer to the following scale:

20-40: Your self-awareness and boundary-setting skills may need improvement. Consider reflecting on your values, goals, and priorities, and seeking guidance or resources to enhance your boundary-setting abilities.

41-60: You have some awareness of your boundaries and self-awareness, but there's room for growth. Keep working on your self-reflection and communication skills to establish and maintain healthier boundaries.

61-80: You have a good understanding of your boundaries and self-awareness, but there may still be areas where you can improve.

Continue to practice self-reflection and assertive communication, and be open to feedback from others.

81-100: You demonstrate strong self-awareness and boundary-setting skills. Continue to cultivate your self-awareness, adjust your boundaries as needed, and maintain open communication with others in the workplace.

The practice of setting and maintaining boundaries is an ongoing journey that necessitates a blend of self-awareness, assertiveness, and resilience. This self-assessment serves as a testament to the importance of acknowledging strengths and identifying areas for improvement in boundary setting, which are integral to both personal and professional development.

Exercise: Boundary Setting and Self-Awareness

1. Can you identify a specific instance at work where you felt overwhelmed or stressed? What was the specific limit that was crossed, and how could you have responded differently?
2. How do your personal values align or clash with your current work environment? How might you establish boundaries that honor your values and goals?
3. Think of a situation where you felt emotionally charged at work. How could you have used emotional intelligence to set or maintain a boundary?
4. How comfortable do you feel advocating for your boundaries at work? What steps can you take to become a stronger advocate for yourself and others?
5. How often do you re-assess your boundaries at work? What triggers or signs indicate that it's time to re-evaluate your boundaries?
6. What is one success you've had in maintaining a work boundary? What did you learn from that experience, and how can you apply that learning moving forward?
7. How has your self-awareness helped or hindered your ability to set boundaries at work? How can you cultivate greater self-awareness

to support effective boundary setting?

8. In what ways do your strengths allow you to maintain healthy boundaries at work? Can you think of a situation where you could have leveraged your strengths more effectively to uphold a boundary?

9. How do your current work boundaries reflect your personal goals? If there is a misalignment, what changes can you make?

10. How have your emotional responses at work informed your boundary setting? What emotional cues could you pay more attention to in future boundary-setting situations?

11. How could you help create a culture that respects boundaries at your workplace? What might be the first step in this process?

12. Can you identify a setback you've experienced in setting or maintaining a boundary at work? What did you learn from this experience, and how can you use this learning to approach future boundary situations?

13. What self-reflection exercises have you found helpful for better boundary-setting?

14. How will you celebrate your successes and learn from setbacks in your boundary-setting journey?

Conclusion

In conclusion, setting boundaries is essential for achieving happiness, productivity and a healthy work-life balance. We spend a significant portion of our lives working, and it is crucial to set boundaries and understand our own worth and value. As we have discussed in this book, boundaries are the limits we set to protect our time, energy, and well-being. Without boundaries, we may find ourselves overworked, stressed, and burnt out.

According to author and researcher Brené Brown, daring to set boundaries is an act of self-love. Setting boundaries means we are willing to risk disappointing others in order to prioritise our own needs. It also means we are not basing our self-worth on others' approval, but rather understanding that we are enough as we are.

When we fail to understand our own worth and value, we may try to attain a sense of worthiness through our work, but this can lead to burnout and a constant need for approval. By understanding our own worth and value, we can gain an awareness and appreciation of our achievements and what we have to offer. This understanding allows us to set boundaries that are aligned with our values, goals, and priorities.

Setting boundaries and showing respect for ourselves can earn us the respect of others and contribute to our overall happiness and productivity. It is important to establish and maintain boundaries in order to make our work experience as comfortable and manageable as possible. By setting boundaries, we can reduce stress, conserve energy, and time, and find joy and peace in our daily lives. By taking control of our work relationships, environment, and job requirements, we can create a more fulfilling and satisfying work experience.

In this book, we have explored different strategies and techniques for setting boundaries, such as setting clear working hours, limiting after-hours communication, and learning to say no to unreasonable demands. We have also discussed the importance of communication, assertiveness, and self-awareness in setting boundaries.

We hope that this book has provided you with valuable insights and tools to set boundaries at work and create a more fulfilling and satisfying work experience. Remember, setting boundaries is an ongoing process, and it takes time and practice to establish and maintain them. Be patient with yourself and trust in your ability to create the work environment that best serves your needs and goals.

References

American Psychological Association. (2017). Stress and technology: Always connected, always stressed. https://www.apa.org/news/press/releases/stress/2017/technology-use

American Psychological Association. (2021). Chronic Work Stress and Health: Research Brief. Retrieved from https://www.apa.org/research/action/chronic-work-stress

Bakker, A. B., Demerouti, E., & Sanz-Vergel, A. I. (2014). Burnout and work engagement: The JD-R approach. Annual Review of Organizational Psychology and Organizational Behavior, 1(1), 389-411.

Banks, S. M., Salovey, P., Greener, S., Rothman, A. J., Moyer, A., Beauvais, J., Epel, E. S., & Major, K. (2010). The effects of message framing on mammography utilization. Health Psychology, 29(4), 415–427. https://doi.org/10.1037/a0020079

Barker, E. (2016). Productivity guilt: Why we feel it and how to overcome it. Psych Central. Retrieved from https://psychcentral.com/blog/productivity-guilt-why-we-feel-it-and-how-to-overcome-it/

Barker, S. (2016). Why You Need to Set Boundaries. Psychology Today. Retrieved from https://www.psychologytoday.com/blog/in-flux/201605/why-you-need-set-boundaries

Bock, C. (2017). Employees' personal information sharing and its impact on emotional exhaustion and burnout. Journal of Business and Psychology, 32(3), 363-376.

Dembe, A. E., Erickson, J. B., Delbos, R. G., & Banks, S. M. (2005). The impact of overtime and long work hours on occupational injuries and illnesses: new evidence from the United States. Journal of Occupational and Environmental Medicine, 47(9), 891-898.

Demerouti, E., Bakker, A. B., Nachreiner, F., & Schaufeli, W. B. (2001). The job demands-resources model of burnout. Journal of Applied Psychology, 86(3), 499-512. https://doi.org/10.1037/0021-9010.86.3.499

Frone, M. R. (2000). Work-family balance. In E. A. Locke (Ed.), Handbook of principles of organizational behavior (pp. 481-497). Wiley.

Gallop. (2020). Employee burnout: Causes and cures. Retrieved from https://www.gallop.com/article/31710/employee-burnout-causes-cures

Gershon, D. (2019). "Hustle culture": A new threat to the well-being of workers? Industrial and Organizational Psychology, 12(2), 111-113. https://doi.org/10.1017/iop.2019.2

Grawitch, M. J., Werth, P. M., & Palmer, S. N. (2018). Research supports the benefits of setting boundaries, indicating that it can improve job satisfaction and reduce the risk of burnout. In J. J. Brien (Ed.), Handbook of work-life integration (pp. 123-145). Publisher.

Greenhaus, J. H., & Beutell, N. J. (1985). Sources of conflict between work and family roles. Academy of Management Review, 10(1), 76-88.

Hofstede, G. (2001). Culture's consequences: Comparing values, behaviors, institutions, and organizations across nations (2nd ed.). Sage.

Kalleberg, A. L. (2018). Good jobs, bad jobs: The rise of polarized and precarious employment systems in the United States, 1970s-2000s. Russell Sage Foundation.

Kossek, E. E., & Lautsch, B. A. (2018). Work–life boundary management and boundary permeability. The Oxford Handbook of Work and Family, 313-330.

Kushlev, K., & Dunn, E. W. (2015). Checking email less frequently reduces stress. Computers in Human Behavior, 43, 220-228. doi:10.1016/j.chb.2014.11.005

Leiter, M. P., & Maslach, C. (2000). Burnout and stress among nurses: Handbook of occupational health psychology. American Psychological Association.

Leiter, M. P., & Maslach, C. (2000). Preventing burnout and building engagement: A complete program for organizational renewal. San Francisco, CA: Jossey-Bass.

Maslach, C., & Leiter, M. P. (2016). Understanding burnout: New models. In Professional burnout: Recent developments in theory and research (pp. 1-16). Routledge.

Maslach, C., Schaufeli, W. B., & Leiter, M. P. (2001). Job burnout. Annual Review of Psychology, 52(1), 397-422. https://doi.org/10.1146/annurev.psych.52.1.397

Mazmanian, M., Orlikowski, W. J., & Yates, J. (2013). The autonomy paradox: The implications of mobile email devices for knowledge professionals. Organization Science, 24(5), 1337-1357. https://doi.org/10.1287/orsc.1120.0799

Nippert-Eng, C. (1996). Calendars and keys: The classification of "home" and "work". Sociological Forum, 11(3), 563-582. https://doi.org/10.1007/BF02408386

Orth, U., Robins, R. W., & Meier, L. L. (2009). Disentangling the effects of low self-esteem and stressful events on depression: Findings from three longitudinal studies. Journal of Personality and Social Psychology, 97(2), 307-321. https://doi.org/10.1037/a0015645

Park, Y., Fritz, C., & Jex, S. M. (2018). Relationships between work-home segmentation and psychological detachment from work: The role of communication technology use at home. Journal of Occupational Health Psychology, 23(4), 537-548. doi:10.1037/ocp0000114

Perlow, L. A. (2017). Sleeping with your smartphone: How to break the 24/7 habit and change the way you work. Harvard Business Review Press.

Pleck, J. H. (1997). Paternal involvement: Levels, sources, and consequences. In M. E. Lamb (Ed.), The role of the father in child development (3rd ed., pp. 66-103). Wiley.

Sparks, K., Cooper, C., Fried, Y., & Shirom, A. (1997). The effects of hours of work on health: A meta-analytic review. Journal of Occupational and Organizational Psychology, 70(4), 391-408. https://doi.org/10.1111/j.2044-8325.1997.tb00661.x

Stoeber, J., & Otto, K. (2006). Positive conceptions of perfectionism: Approaches, evidence, challenges. Personality and Social Psychology Review, 10(4), 295-319.

Stoeber, J., & Otto, K. (2006). Positive conceptions of perfectionism: Approaches, evidence, challenges. Personality and Social Psychology Review, 10(4), 295-319.

Stoeber, J., & Rennert, D. (2008). Perfectionism in school teachers: Relations with stress appraisals, coping styles, and burnout. Anxiety, Stress & Coping, 21(1), 37-53. https://doi.org/10.1080/10615800701562741

Turkle, S. (2015). Reclaiming conversation: The power of talk in a digital age. Penguin Press.

Virtanen, M., Stansfeld, S. A., Fuhrer, R., Ferrie, J. E., & Kivimäki, M. (2012). Overtime work as a predictor of major depressive episode: a 5-year follow-up of the Whitehall II study. PLoS One, 7(1), e30719.

Vorderer, P., Klimmt, C., & Ritterfeld, U. (2004). Enjoyment: At the heart of media entertainment. Communication Theory, 14(4), 388–408. https://doi.org/10.1111/j.1468-2885.2004.tb00325.x

World Health Organization. (2019). Burn-out an "occupational phenomenon": International Classification of Diseases. Retrieved from https://www.who.int/news/item/28-05-2019-burn-out-an-occupational-phenomenon-international-classification-of-diseases

Zomorodi, M. (2015). Bored and brilliant: How spacing out can unlock your most productive and creative self. St. Martin's Press.